THE BLACK PRESS

AND THE STRUGGLE

FOR CIVIL RIGHTS

THE BLACK PRESS

AND THE STRUGGLE

FOR CIVIL RIGHTS

BY CARL SENNA

THE AFRICAN-AMERICAN EXPERIENCE
FRANKLIN WATTS
NEW YORK   CHICAGO   LONDON   TORONTO   SYDNEY

Photographs copyright ©: UPI/Bettmann Newsphotos: p. 1; Talladega College, AL: p. 2; Library of Congress: pp. 3, 5, 7, 10; Schlesinger Library, Radcliffe College: p. 4 top; New York Public Library: pp. 4 bottom (Picture Collection), 6, 9 (both Schomburg Center for Research in Black Culture), 11, 16 (both Special Collections); Gamma-Liaison/Fox: p. 8; National Archives: p. 12 top; The Bettmann Archive: p. 13 top; U.S. Marine Corps Photo: p. 13 bottom; AP/Wide World Photos: pp. 14 top, 15; Archive Photos, NYC: p. 14 bottom.

Library of Congress Cataloging-in-Publication Data

Senna, Carl, 1944–
    The black press and the struggle for civil rights / by Carl Senna.
        p.   cm.—(The African-American experience)
    Includes bibliographical references and index.
    Summary: An account of the black press from the first black newspaper to the integration of black journalists into the mainstream of American journalism.
    ISBN 0-531-11036-2
    1. Afro-American press—History—Juvenile literature.   2. Afro-Americans—Civil rights—Juvenile literature.   3. United States— Race relations—History—Juvenile literature.
    [1. Afro-American press—History.   2. Afro-Americans— Civil rights.   3. Newspapers— History.]   I. Title.   II. Series.
    PN4882.5.s46   1993
    071'.308996—dc20   93-17558 CIP AC

First Paperback Edition 1994
0-531-15693-1

CONTENTS

for A.M.S. (r.i.p.)

PREFACE

It is not surprising if the Negro turns with more than ordinary devotion to the printed page. To him it is an institution peculiarly embodying his group life, something like his church or his lodge, but even more like some public work of art symbolizing his aspiration.

—Frederick G. Detweiler,
The Negro Press in the United States[1]

Gunnar Myrdal, a renowned Swedish social scientist, observed in the 1940s that the black press not only is the second most important black institution after the black church but is a unique development in the growth of American newspaper publishing. This account begins with the first black newspaper and concludes with the integration of black journalists into the mainstream of American journalism.

By choice as well by necessity, the black press began largely in news related to the struggle of blacks in America to secure racial equality. Since then, the press has continued the role of promoting civil rights for blacks, highlighting news about blacks who are either notorious or famous, and "race angling" the news, which has led to charges of racial obsession. In 1986, for example, *The Amsterdam News* reported the spacecraft *Challenger* disaster with a headline identifying only the black astronaut who perished among several casualties. The racial angle both served readers who racially identified themselves as a people and preserved the market for news of social, political, and economic "progress" in racial terms.

After World War II, *Ebony* magazine publisher John H. Johnson was one of the first major black publishers to view the civil rights movement with mixed emotions. For a long time he feared losing black customers to white controlled journals with interracial appeal. But probably every black publisher at one time or another has sensed the irony of a black editorial that simultaneously advocated racial integration and encouraged racial loyalty in the buying habits of black readers. One of the economic paradoxes, indeed, of the black press has been that it stood to gain readers—in the short term, at least—whether it promoted the black nationalist slogan "Buy Black" or upheld the integrationist slogan "We shall overcome." Traditionally, any news coverage from a black point of view has won black patronage.

A number of prominent black journalists have been leaders in civil rights and in other fields. The roster of current and past civil rights leaders who were journalists could read like a *Who's Who* of black history. Nobel Peace Prize winner and former United Nations diplomat Ralph Bunche; National Association for the Advancement of Colored People (NAACP) secretaries W. E. B. Du Bois, Walter White, and Roy Wilkins; and labor organizer Bayard Rustin—all figured prominently in the 1940s–1960s movement for civil rights, but their involvement in the black press was mainly as columnists. Journalists have included educators, fiction writers, and poets (Ann Petry, Richard Wright, Harold Cruse, James Baldwin, Langston Hughes, Roi Ottley, and James Alan McPherson, to name only a small number).

Currently, blacks work on every major commercial television news program. Stars include Ed Bradley of CBS's "Sixty Minutes," Jesse Jackson of CNN's "Both Sides with Jesse Jackson," NBC's "Today" host Bryant Gumbel, Tony Brown of "Tony Brown's Journal," CNN network anchors Bernard Shaw and Lynn Vaughn, National Public Radio's Phylliss Crockett, ABC network's Carole Simpson, and NBC's Ann Curry and Deborah Roberts. Talk show stars include Oprah Winfrey, Montel Williams, and Arsenio Hall. National newspapers like *The New York Times, The Washington Post*, and *USA Today* publish the work of black columnists, executives, and editors, such as the syndicated columnists William Raspberry, Carl Rowan, Dorothy Pulliam, Earl Caldwell, Roger Wilkins, and Thomas Sowell; *The Washington Post*'s Juan Williams; the Pulitzer Prize-winning commentator Clarence Page; *USA Today*'s Barbara Reynolds; *The New York Times*'s Roger Wilkins, Brent Staples, Lee Daniels, Sheila Rule, and others.

I wish to acknowledge the generous assistance of the following libraries: the staff of the Providence College Library, the Providence Public Library Special Collections, Brown University's Rockefeller Library, and the Mortensen Library's African American Special Collections of the University of Hartford, Connecticut; the New Bedford, Fall River, and Westport, Massachusetts, libraries; the Hartford and West Hartford Public libraries of Hartford, Connecticut; Pam Johnson of *The Ithaca Journal*; Ed Bradley of CBS News; Earl Graves of *Black Enterprise Magazine*; and all the other people who helped me with the development of this book. And finally, I wish to thank Constance Pohl for her editorial direction in completing the manuscript.

I
THE BIRTH OF THE BLACK PRESS

We wish to plead our cause. Too long have others spoken for us.

—Opening editorial,
Freedom's Journal, 1827[1]

On Friday, March 16, 1827, the first issue of *Freedom's Journal* appeared on the streets of New York City. The United States had been a republic for nearly fifty years. Commerce and the number of newspapers and magazines had increased. New publications were appearing nearly every week.

At first glance newspaper customers simply would have noted that one more paper was competing for their attention, bought their regular newspapers, and forgotten the new paper. But a curious browser of *Freedom's Journal* would have noted that the paper was strikingly unlike any other on the newsstands. The browser would have been startled to see that news in *Freedom's Journal* was all about African American life, and that announcements and advertisements were directed to blacks. Above all, the editorial on the front page indicated in the boldest tone that the publisher and editor of the paper were black, defiantly and proudly black.

Freedom's Journal was the first collective effort of a black community to protest racism on a frequent basis. As the front page editorial declared:

We wish to plead our own cause. Too long have others spoken for us. Too long has the publick been deceived by misrepresentations, in things which concern us dearly, though in the estimation of some mere trifles; for though there are many in society who exercise towards us benevolent feelings; still (with sorrow we confess it) there are others who make it their business to enlarge upon the least trifle. . . .[2]

In New York City, free blacks, including women and children, were subject to harassment on the streets. Lynchings of blacks were common occurrences. Worse, many whites approved of the American Colonization Society's proposal to remove all blacks from the United States to Africa and South America. Even traditional friends of black freedom, the abolitionists William Lloyd Garrison; Benjamin Lundy, author of *The Genius of Universal Emancipation*; and Gerrit Smith, advocated that all blacks be emancipated in order to facilitate their return to Africa.

More threatening to free blacks than colonization was the racist image of blacks daily circulated and sustained by white newspapers. It seemed that nearly all white newspapers presented stereotypes of blacks as inarticulate, ignorant, subhumans, often with immoral and criminal qualities. In the words of one white racist journalist, blacks aspired to no other [condition] *than that of base and beastlike slavery. These black people are by nature of an exceedingly low and groveling disposition. They have no trait of character that is lovely or admirable. They are not high-minded, enterprising, nor prudent . . . that, in addition to the black and baneful color of the negro, there are numerous other defects, physical, mental, and moral, which clearly mark him, when coupled with the white man as a very different and inferior creature.*[3]

Freedom's Journal's immediate goal was to oppose Mordecai Manuel Noah, the eminent Jewish publisher of the influential white newspaper *The New York Enquirer.* To encourage slavery and discourage black freedom, Noah consistently vilified blacks in every possible form of human degradation in print.[4] To counter Noah's propaganda, John B. Russwurm, the Reverend Samuel E. Cornish, and other free blacks met in the New York City home of Boston Crummell, a respected leader in the small free black community. After a series of discussions the leaders decided to publish a newspaper; they selected two of the youngest and best educated men among them to accomplish the job, Cornish and Russwurm.

The Reverend Samuel E. Cornish was born in Delaware in 1795 of free black parents. He attended Free African schools in Philadelphia and New York City and on graduation became a minister. He then organized the first black Presbyterian church in New York City.

Russwurm was from Jamaica, the son of a white planter and a slave woman. His father had secretly educated Russwurm in Canada under the name of John Brown. When the planter's white wife learned of Russwurm's paternity, she arranged for Russwurm to adopt the planter's name. Later she financed Russwurm's education, and he graduated from Bowdoin College in 1826.

An extremely practical man, Russwurm, the paper's junior editor and business manager, complemented the idealistic and uncompromising Cornish.

In the paper's prospectus—an announcement and description of the new business—Cornish and Russwurm wrote:

We shall ever regard the Constitution of the United States as our polar star. Pledged to no party, we shall endeavor to urge our brethren to use their rights to the elective franchise as free citizens. It shall never be our object to court controversy though we must at all times consider ourselves as champions in defense of oppressed humanity. Daily slandered, we think that there ought to be some channel of communication between us and the public, through which a single voice may be heard, in defense of five hundred thousand free people of colour. Too often has injustice been heaped upon us, when our only defense was an appeal to the Almighty, but we believe that the time has now arrived, when the calumnies of our enemies should be refuted by forcible arguments. . . .[5]

The first editorial set the tone the black press would take up to the present day. Civil rights and the ballot were demanded immediately: "The civil rights of a people being of the greatest value, it shall ever be our duty to vindicate our brethren, when oppressed; and to lay the case before the publick."6

With respect to readership interest, the paper declared, its coverage extended to

useful knowledge of every kind, and every-thing that relates to Africa [and to espouse the cause of the slaves who] are our kindred by all the ties of nature. . . . [The editorial stressed the importance of education]: Education being an object of the highest importance to the wel-fare of society, we shall endeavour to present just and adequate views of it, and to urge upon our brethren the necessity and expediency of training their children, while young, to habits of industry. . . .

It is our wish to make our Journal a me-dium of intercourse between our brethren in the different states of this great confederacy; that through its columns an expression of our sentiments, on many interesting subjects which concern us, may be offered to the pub-lick; that plans which apparently are benefi-cial may be candidly discussed and properly weighed; if worthy, receive our cordial appro-bation; if not, our marked disapprobation.7

Freedom's Journal resembled a magazine more than a newspaper. Only two of the sixteen columns cov-ered actual foreign and domestic news. The other columns were devoted to black human interest fea-tures: "Memoirs" of New Bedford black Captain Paul Cuffe, a report on the illegal imprisonment of a poet, articles on "Common Schools of New York," "The

Church and the Auction Block," "A True Story," an essay on "The Effect of Sight Upon a Person Born Blind," "On Choosing a Wife by Proxy," antislavery notices, entertainment news, variety notices, notices of marriages and deaths, and court trials and commercial advertisements on the last page.

As historian Lerone Bennett, Jr., notes, in featuring blacks as parents, workers, and social creatures, Cornish and Russwurm challenged the racial stereotype of blacks fostered by the white press. The paper was published weekly on Friday at 5 Varick Street in Manhattan, a center of newspaper publishing and printing. Subscriptions came from as far away as Canada, England, and Haiti. Its correspondents included James Forten, Sr., a Revolutionary War naval inventor, abolitionist, and philanthropist; radical publicist David Walker; and Richard Allen, founder of the African Methodist Episcopal Church. Features on black poet Phyllis Wheatley, Haitian liberator Toussaint L'Ouverture, and other black leaders were given wide circulation. Race pride was a reluctant emphasis, forced out of "strong necessity" by racism, but the interests of the paper touched nonracial areas of literature and science as well.

The immediate practical effect of *Freedom's Journal* was to expose blacks as far south as Virginia and Maryland to antislavery writings, promoting hope for the slave and resistance to slavery. The paper was considered subversive literature in the South. Blacks were punished severely for possessing copies. But the paper's influence reached far beyond its small number of readers. On July 4, 1827, the New York legislature emancipated all slaves in the state, an event that sent shock waves through southern states. On that day, *Freedom's Journal* received a number of testimonials and toasts to the paper's role in persuading the legislature to free New York's slaves. At one public dinner in Fredericksburg, Virginia, free blacks declared in a toast to *Freedom's Journal* that Virginia, and her sister slave states, ought to show to the people of colour on the 4th of July 1827, that they have approved of the example set them by the legislature of New York.

Whites in the South, however, grew more sympathetic to proslavery President Andrew Jackson, elected in 1828 by a wide margin. And even though New York had emancipated slaves in the state, New York still abrogated or curtailed black voting rights, joining Ohio, New Jersey, and Pennsylvania in their ban on black suffrage.

Later in 1827, Cornish resigned from the paper, wishing to devote his energies to promote Free African Schools, privately run schools for free black children in the North. When Russwurm took over, he donated the paper's editorials to expatriation, or "Back to Africa," a strategy unpopular with most black abolitionists.

Russwurm's expatriation scheme was the death of the newspaper. Sales, investment, and advertisement dropped. On March 21, 1828, Russwurm changed the name of the paper to *Rights of All*. Although the paper was published for two more years, it sometimes missed an issue and circulation never rose enough to support expenses.

The paper was not helped by the notoriety of its writers. As free blacks became more desperate, some of them became more militant. In 1829, *Rights of All* writer David Walker, a free black newspaper agent from North Carolina, issued a fiery pamphlet, *Walker's Appeal*, urging blacks to free themselves by violence: "Remember, Americans, that we must and shall be free and enlightened as you are, will you wait until we shall, under God, obtain our liberty by the crushing arm of power? Will it not be dreadful for you?"[8] *Walker's Appeal* caused a bounty to be placed on his head, reducing his freedom of action as an agent for *Rights of All*.

In 1829, Russwurm received his master's degree from Bowdoin College and he resigned from the paper. Soon after he graduated, he set sail for Liberia, where he founded the *Liberia Herald*. The day Russwurm resigned from *Rights of All*, Cornish resumed editorship of the paper. Despite the efforts of Cornish to win back former advertisers and readers, the *Journal* began to slide into bankruptcy.

Cornish would later become the first editor of *The Colored American* (see pages 28–30), sharing his editorial authority with three other coeditors. Cornish, however, was never a team player, and he so often clashed with his colleagues and the publisher on editorial positions that he stayed at the paper barely six months. Nevertheless, he contributed freelance columns long after leaving.

Though Cornish worked on a number of antislavery committees, he was oddly enough a champion of industrial-trade school education for blacks. Discriminatory work laws divided black and white workers, frustrating abolitionists. Writing in the September 2, 1839 *Colored American*, Samuel Cornish called on black slaves and underpaid white laborers to make common cause in "anarchy, bloodshed and rapine."[9] Opposing expatriation and compromises on civil rights, he was nevertheless a conservative on full and immediate equality. He discouraged blacks from higher education and argued against establishing a black elite. Many blacks criticized his educational proposals as demeaning. Nonetheless, Cornish was partly responsible for the first black press prior to the Civil War.

Russwurm had left journalism for good after working on *Freedom's Journal/Rights of All*. He served as school superintendent and governor of the Maryland Colony at Cape Palmas, Liberia. He died in his beloved Africa on June 9, 1851. The two founders of the black press in America had lived long enough to link the struggle for civil rights to *Freedom's Journal*, the first African American paper. The honor of being first could never be shared, no matter how many imitators the paper would leave to continue the struggle.

II
THE STRUGGLE AGAINST SLAVERY (1831–1841)

HISTORICAL OVERVIEW, 1831–1841

As the country debated whether slavery should be permitted in new states entering the Union, violence flared with casualties on both sides. Prominent slaveholders South Carolina Senator John C. Calhoun and Kentucky Senator Henry Clay argued that with the growing numbers of free blacks in the North, white support for slavery would diminish. In 1830, when David Walker, a writer for *Rights of All*, mysteriously vanished without a trace, many of his friends suspected he had been silenced by bounty hunters. While many blacks dreaded bounty hunters and a return to slavery, the mood among many whites in cities and towns along the Eastern Seaboard was one of fear, not of the British, nor of Indian attack, but of slave revolt.

On August 21, 1831 (the year *Rights of All* ceased publication), Virginia slave Nat Turner, as though fulfilling David Walker's ominous warning to whites of black vengeance, led the bloodiest slave rebellion in the country. Before he was captured and executed, he had killed fifty-seven whites. After Turner's rebellion, discrimination against free blacks worsened, especially in the South. Abolitionists in the North and in the South, in the White House and on street corners, were suddenly besieged by white proslavery arguments. Even abolitionist Lydia Child objected to black's social equality with whites.

In 1831, Professor Thomas R. Dew of William and Mary College in Virginia published a popular defense of slavery, pointing out that the Bible sanctioned slavery and that

we cannot get rid of slavery without producing a greater injury to both the master and slaves. . . . Everyone acquainted with Southern slaves knows that the slave rejoices in the elevation and prosperity of his master. . . . A merrier being does not exist on the face of the globe than the Negro slave of the United States.[1]

In response, abolitionists stepped up their campaign in northern states. "In your sufferings I participate,"[2] declared twenty-six-year-old William Lloyd Garrison, the white publisher of *The Liberator*, first issued January 1, 1831. Cornish and four hundred other black abolitionists subscribed to Garrison's paper, which included five black managers on the paper's board. Levi Coffin, an Indiana Quaker and banker, shared Garrison's sentiments and helped establish the Underground Railroad, a network of private homes used to assist fugitive slaves to escape and elude recapture.

Responding to Professor Dew's defense of slavery, New England poet John Greenleaf Whittier published a pamphlet in 1833, *Justice and Expediency*, calling for "immediate abolition of slavery; an immediate acknowledgement of the great truth that man cannot hold property in man."[3]

In 1833, Theodore Dwight Weld of Connecticut joined two wealthy New York merchants, Arthur and Lewis Tappan, and free blacks in Philadelphia to establish the American Anti-Slavery Society. The need for the society could not have been greater. The following year, Prudence Crandall, a white teacher in Canterbury, Connecticut, was forced by a white mob to close her school for blacks. Tension between the North and South delighted abolitionists. For free blacks, the regional conflict had the added virtue of paralyzing the white proslavery minority in the North. Instead of lying low, free blacks began a strident publishing campaign to exacerbate white division over slavery.

Freedom's Journal, though now silent, had spawned a number of successors to continue the struggle for abolition and civil rights. Most of the "papers" contained little other than opinions and were published irregularly, on a monthly, quarterly, or biannual basis. During that period, when as many as twenty-four newspapers were published by blacks, the first black magazines appeared: *The National Reformer* and the *Mirror of Liberty*.

THE MIRROR OF LIBERTY, 1838–1842

David Ruggles, one of the first black abolitionist publishers after Cornish and Russwurm, had started his working career as a salesman advertising food products for grocers, and even then he had been hardly timid about expressing his political ideas. In the fall and winter issues of *Freedom's Journal* of 1828 a Ruggles ad appeared offering "free sugars . . . manufactured by free people, not by slaves."[4] The ad's political message signaled his early interest in the antislavery cause.

Ruggles was described by one contemporary as "of unmixed blood, which clearly showed the possibilities of a race of people, some of whom were slaves and others free but without the right of franchisement, and with no means of elevation."[5]

Born in Norwich, Connecticut, in 1810, Ruggles had been educated in the elementary public schools, but he left home for New York City at the age of seventeen.

In the 1830s, Ruggles became the secretary of the New York Vigilance Committee, a job which directly exposed him to proslavery violence. He often searched New York harbors and forced his way on board slave ships to rescue kidnapped freed slaves or arrested runaways. In some cases, when he could not directly liberate a slave from a New York master, he sued the owners. His home became a shelter along the Underground Railroad and once was the refuge of the great runaway slave Frederick Douglass! So notorious was his agitation that slave catchers attacked his home, hoping to capture or to destroy him. Fortunately, Ruggles escaped injury, but during the course of work for the Underground Railroad he often changed his address to throw the proslavery forces off his tracks.

Believing that the mighty power of the American press could end slavery, Ruggles contributed articles to white and black newspapers and wrote pamphlets in the antislavery cause.

A contemporary of Ruggles said he had "those qualities of keen perception, deep thought, and originality, that mark the critic and man of letters . . . keen and witty,—always logical,—sending his arrows directly at his opponent."[6]

In 1833 David Ruggles gave up the grocery business to become a traveling salesman for the New York *Emancipator*, an abolitionist newspaper. At this time, Ruggles began his publishing career, and soon he made a reputation as a publicist, journalist, and activist in the antislavery crusade.

In 1834, Ruggles attempted to use a public library and was denied entrance because of his color. Thus he learned that most libraries, or reading rooms, as libraries were called, refused to admit blacks. His reaction was to open his own private library, a subscription reading room and a bookstore, which let readers borrow books. His circulating library combined advertising, job printing, picture framing, and bookbinding. For a yearly membership fee of $2.75, blacks, he declared "who are despised for their complexion and refused admission to public reading rooms generally, may enjoy the rich benefits which such an establishment furnishes."[7] His library offered the major daily newspapers as well as antislavery literature, which he aggressively distributed, much to the annoyance of proslavery officials.

In 1835, President Andrew Jackson appealed to Congress to stifle abolitionists like Ruggles, whom he described as "misguided persons engaged in these unconstitutional and wicked attempts. . . ."[8] South Carolina Governor George McDuffie, reasoned that blacks "have all the qualities that fit them for slaves, and not one of those that would fit them to be freemen. They are utterly unqualified not only for rational freedom but for self-government of any kind."[9]

Jackson's appeal to silence abolitionists was ineffective, as were proslavery arguments. But when abolitionists like Ruggles tried to petition Congress to end slavery in the nation's capital, southern and northern conservatives in Congress imposed a gag rule on abolitionist petitions.

Senator John C. Calhoun unsuccessfully urged the Senate to adopt a gag rule similar to the congressional procedure, insisting that "Abolition and the Union cannot coexist,"[10] and that abolitionism was dragging the regions into war. Many wealthy northerners agreed with Calhoun, arguing as one merchant did, that slavery "is not a matter of principle with us. It is a matter of business necessity. We cannot afford to let [abolitionism] succeed."[11]

For the abolitionist press of any color, it was a dangerous time. In 1835, William Lloyd Garrison was trapped in his newspaper office, hauled outside, and humiliated by a white gang. In 1837, white abolitionist publisher Elijah Lovejoy was murdered, and his press in Alton, Illinois, was thrown into the river.

Ruggles, meanwhile, experienced two humiliating episodes of racial discrimination in New England, once when he was denied first-class passage on a steamboat and again when he was ejected from a seat in a whites-only rail coach—all within the same month. To add insult to injury, he found that his complaints were not admitted in a court of law, segregation being legal, nor did he have a press to voice his indignation. Thus he became publisher of the quarterly *Mirror of Liberty*, which was published in the years 1838–1842.

His *Mirror of Liberty* was a sixteen-page magazine largely devoted to essays attacking slavery, racial discrimination, and colonization. As publisher and editor, Ruggles proclaimed that the *Mirror of Liberty* "is a free and independent journal—its editor is an unmuzzled man, who goes for freedom of speech and the liberty of the press."[12] The journal's motto was "Liberty is the word for me—above all, liberty."[13] Newspapers all over the East Coast reprinted articles and opinions from the *Mirror*.

A white paper in Ohio hailed Ruggles for displaying a rare "ability and talent seldom to be found, even among those who call themselves the better part of creation."[14] But critics, especially white southern editors such as one Virginia writer, reviled the *Mirror* as "an incendiary periodical" with "a disposition to encourage lynch law" and Ruggles as simply "a poor deluded negro."[15]

In July 1841 the *Mirror* published a poem by John Greenleaf Whittier, probably the first time a poem has ever been headlined on a news periodical's front page as an "Extra."

Many white abolitionists who contributed to the *Mirror* had already won distinction outside the antislavery cause. But white writers greatly outrepresented black writers in the *Mirror*'s columns; over 90 percent of blacks were still illiterate. Nevertheless, blacks organized public meetings in New York, Hartford, New Bedford, and Boston to raise subscriptions and donations for the *Mirror*. Despite such efforts to keep the paper in circulation, the mounting costs of publication caused the paper to fold in 1842.

THE COLORED AMERICAN, 1837–1842

In January 1837, Philip A. Bell founded *The Weekly Advocate* in New York City, but after two months he decided that he needed a racially identifiable tag to distinguish it from the standard abolitionist papers. So Bell renamed his four-page, four-column weekly paper *The Colored American*, and named Cornish the first editor.

The Colored American's billing policy was highly conservative. Subscribers were charged $1.50 per year payable in advance of delivery. The subscription terms reflected either the poor credit risk of most subscribers, or an unusual degree of financial caution of the paper's principal investor, Robert Sears of Toronto, Ontario, a white man described as "a warm friend to the race."[16]

A sensational and successful slave revolt, led by Joseph Cinque, on the ship *Amistad* in 1839 infuriated the southern congressional leadership but was duly described in both the *Mirror* and *The Colored American* as a warning of impending civil war.

The Colored American proved to be a formidable response to white proslavery arguments. In 1840, for instance, Calhoun argued that slavery improved blacks, "not only physically, but morally and intellectually."[17] He cited statistics showing that slaves were less inclined to insanity than freedmen, that slaves outlived freedmen, and that there were nineteen cases of black insanity in six Maine towns. *The Colored American*'s Dr. James McCune Smith, a respected scholar and physician, demolished Senator Calhoun's argument and his statistics, for as Smith discovered, the census indicated only one black living in the area. Smith replied sarcastically, "To make 19 crazy men out of one man, is pretty fair calculation. . . . Freedom has not made us mad; it has strengthened our minds by throwing us upon our own resources and has bound us to American institutions with a tenacity which nothing but death can overcome."[18]

Even though *The Colored American* ceased publication in 1842, Calhoun had been correct in assessing the black mood. Blacks everywhere were becoming bolder in challenging slavery. Another successful slave revolt aboard the ship *Creole* in 1841, led by Madison Washington, only confirmed white fears.

Reflecting the growth and confidence of black freedmen, the *African Methodist Episcopal Review*, a black journal, began publication in 1841 and immediately championed emancipation, a radical departure (with the exception of Quaker journals) from the silence on slavery of mainline white church publications.

III

THE STRUGGLE AGAINST SLAVERY (1842–1849)

During the early 1840s, as antislavery activists in the North became bolder in challenging the fugitive slave laws, abolitionists became more accepting of violence as a means of emancipation. One historian notes that New York philanthropist Gerrit Smith, in his January 1842 Liberty party convention "Address to the Slaves of the United States," all but declared "war against the South."[1] A year later William Lloyd Garrison called on slaves to "wage war against" the South, "to wade through their blood, if necessary, to secure your own freedom."[2]

The new white abolitionist attitude on violence was shared by free blacks, who considered slavery a source of the racial discrimination they faced. At an 1843 convention of free blacks in Buffalo, New York, the Reverend Samuel Davis called for armed attack on slavery: "No other hope is left us, but in our own exertions and an appeal to the God of armies."[3] Although the sentiment troubled many blacks, the

Reverend Henry Highland Garnet, associated with *The National Watchman* and *The Clarion* newspapers, followed Davis with a fiery call to arms, "Brethren, arise, arise! Strike for your lives and liberties. Now is the day and the hour."[4] Garnet's motion to support slave uprisings, however, was opposed as too extreme by fellow delegate Frederick Douglass, and the motion was defeated.

THE MYSTERY

Black newspapers appeared in a number of northern states. New York led in the number of black newspapers, and Pennsylvania was a close second. Race relations in Pittsburgh in 1843 in particular resembled the bitter race relations in New York City, when John Russwurm and Samuel Cornish had been forced to create *Freedom's Journal*. Pittsburgh blacks were unable to find a white paper willing to publish their opinions on slavery or publish letters by blacks on other subjects.

In 1843, a bright young black resident of Pittsburgh and a former aide to Frederick Douglass so bitterly resented censorship of blacks that he decided to publish his own newspaper. His name was Martin Robison Delany, later Dr. Martin R. Delany, a graduate of Harvard College and the first black graduate of Harvard Medical School. His weekly paper, a quarterly, was called *The Mystery*.

Delany paid for the paper out of his own pocket for the first nine months of its existence. His association with the paper, however, came to a grinding halt as a result of a lawsuit. He became the only black editor in the period from 1827 to 1870 fined for libel, that is, intentional printing of untruths about someone so as to harm his or her reputation.

Delany's editorials were especially critical of white cruelty to slaves. He actually named whites whom he condemned and ridiculed. Clearly, the white judge in his case did not share Delany's hostility to white slave owners. And as a result of his legal expenses, Delany could no longer afford to operate the paper by himself, even though his friends organized a subscription drive and succeeded in paying the fine.

THE RAM'S HORN

In 1841, four years after his *Mirror of Liberty* ceased publication, David Ruggles began the *Genius of Freedom*, which was published from 1845 to 1847. But the *Genius of Freedom* had neither the extensive circulation nor the influence of his *Mirror of Liberty*. The void left by the *Mirror*'s focus on civil rights and antislavery activities was filled by *The Ram's Horn*, a newspaper published in New York City.

New York's Constitution had a "Colored Clause," relating to voting qualifications in public elections. In order to vote, African American males had to own at least $250 worth of real estate and to have paid all back property taxes. Yet white males twenty years old voted without any property qualification. In 1846, civil rights activists persuaded the legislature to offer a ballot to repeal the "Colored Clause." In the referendum campaign, a popular white newspaper, the New York *Sun*, urged readers to keep the clause by voting "No." Willis A. Hodges, a free black, wrote a letter to the editor opposing the *Sun*'s position.

Unlike white readers who wrote letters published in the *Sun*, Hodges was required to pay the paper fifteen dollars before his letter was printed. The paper modified the letter and ran it as an advertisement. Hodges protested the misrepresentation of his position, only to be told by the editor, "The *Sun* shines for all white men, and not for colored men."[5] The editor told Hodges that a black newspaper was the proper place for advocating black equality.

In 1846, with only the infrequently published *Genius of Freedom*, New York City was for all practical purposes without a regular black publication. As a result, Hodges and a white friend, Thomas Van Rensselaer, formed a publishing partnership in October 1846, bringing out three thousand copies of *The Ram's Horn*. The paper's motto proclaimed, "We are men, and therefore interested in whatever concerns men."[6]

Hodges reported that he had earned the money to publish the paper from two months of whitewashing. Published at 141 Fulton Street, the paper charged $1.50 for an annual subscription in New York. The paper listed Frederick Douglass, who had become a popular and respected author since his autobiography's publication in 1845, as editor, but he had little to do with the actual editing of the paper. Hodges and Van Rensselaer really prepared the paper for publication. As one historian put it, "Douglass, while he did little writing for *The Ram's Horn*, was then so highly popular, that no paper was considered of much importance without the name of Douglass connected with it."[7]

A number of events accelerated the march toward war, in particular, the incorporation of Texas into the Union as a slave state in 1845 and the War with Mexico (1846–1848). The prospect of Texas's becoming a haven for fugitive slaves did not appeal to the South, and southern senators like John C. Calhoun quickly secured protection for slavery in the new Texas territory. Already, however, the prospect for further annexations of California and the Southwest kept an acrimonious debate alive in the Congress. Should the newcomers be slave or free? Since Mexico's abolition of slavery in 1829, white Texan slaveholders had wanted the United States to annex the territory so as to protect slavery. Abolitionists, of course, opposed annexation for the very same reason, arguing as did Jabez Delano Hammond, "Every addition of a slave state increases the danger of foreign invasion, and domestic insurrection, and thereby weakens the nation."[8]

Not only did Calhoun argue that slaves were protected property, he also insisted that every state had a right to protect its citizens' property anywhere in the North or in the new territories. Northerners like Senators Salmon P. Chase and William H. Seward asserted the contrary—that new territories must be free of the "slave power."[9] And, of course, antislavery leaders maintained that slavery was illegal on either free or slave soil. A war of words ensued over the issue of territorial status, as well as civil rights for freedmen.

Typically, the focus on regional issues offended some black nationalist leaders. In *The Ram's Horn* a contribution to this debate was the circular reprinted in volume 1, number 43, November 5, 1847, from the black nationalist preacher the Reverend Alexander Crummel, dated April 19, 1846: "The rising antislavery feeling of the north confines itself almost entirely to the interests and rights of the white race, with an almost utter disregard of the Afro-Americans; which tendency is dangerous to us and should be changed."[10]

The regional nature of the debate, however, increased. When the United States went to war with Mexico in 1846, slaves on a Louisiana plantation cheered at news of Mexican victories, according to reports by freedman Solomon Northrup. Abolitionist legislators meanwhile quietly attempted to undermine the extension of slavery resulting from the war. In 1847, Congressman David Wilmot proposed that any territory acquired from Mexico be free of slavery, but his motion was defeated in Congress. The Wilmot Proviso's defeat enraged black abolitionist Charles Remond, and in a widely reported 1847 address in Massachusetts, he abandoned his opposition to Garnet's call for slave insurrection. The influential and proabolitionist Boston *Daily Whig* newspaper called Remond a "traitor to the country, to the Constitution, to Humanity."[11] Even Ellis Gray Loring, a proper Bostonian abolitionist with strong ties to Garrison, appealed, albeit unsuccessfully, to the Anti-Slavery Society to repudiate Remond. Internal divisions hurt black papers as well.

Eighteen months after the first issue of *The Ram's Horn* appeared, Hodges and his partner quarreled, Hodges quit, and the paper ceased publication. Demise of *The Ram's Horn* followed a pattern characteristic of black papers of the period. As one contemporary noted in a commentary on *The Ram's Horn*: "Before the war, few newspapers were published by Afro-Americans. Here and there, a man more intelligent, more venturesome, more affluent than his fellows, turned to journalism as the most effective means of pleading for the abolition of slavery; but his funds would be soon wasted and the issue of his paper would be stopped."[12]

Despite the costs, personal and otherwise, black publications became increasingly necessary as instruments of propaganda. Public debate over whether territories such as Texas would be admitted to the union as slave or free states gave new impetus to black newspapers.

In the presidential election of 1848, the Free Soil

party, the powerful third party composed of antislavery and other radical elements, ran Martin Van Buren against General Zachary Taylor, the hero of the Mexican War. The platform of the Free-Soilers was "Free soil, free speech, free labor and free men."[13] Taylor won the election, but the Free-Soilers under Van Buren made a respectable showing at the polls.

A major case of school discrimination followed in the next year. Sarah C. Roberts, the five-year-old daughter of abolitionist Benjamin Roberts, had to walk a half-mile every day past five white schools to a black school because she and other blacks were barred from Boston's all-white public schools. In 1849 Benjamin sued the city for discrimination on behalf of black children and his daughter. Although Roberts lost the first court challenge to Boston school segregation, his attorney Charles Sumner, who argued Sarah's case before the Massachusetts Supreme Court, pleaded a new legal doctrine, that the Constitution required "equality before the law."[14] Sumner's phrase would define the goal of the American civil rights movement from then on. Abolitionists, enraged already, were quick to react to the legal defeats of the Wilmot Proviso and the Roberts case.

THE SLAVE TELEGRAPH

In the South, free blacks could not operate a press, nor could their white allies. But over the course of the past fifty years a "grapevine" or "slave telegraph" had broadcast news by word-of-mouth of an "Underground Railroad," carrying slaves North to freedom. Brave escaped slaves like Harriet Tubman and Sojourner Truth who sneaked into the South and led slaves to freedom used the "grapevine" and a series of underground "stations" in the homes of sympathetic whites. But word-of-mouth kinds of communication could neither advocate nor propagate arguments against the slave trade. To cover wide areas and to reach mass numbers of people required a publication.

IV

FREDERICK DOUGLASS AND *THE NORTH STAR*

William Lloyd Garrison, Wendell Phillips, and other white abolitionists had tried to discourage potential black publishers from starting newspapers. But the advice had fallen on deaf ears, mainly because the abolitionist message continued to incite slaves like Frederick Douglass, the greatest of the black publishers, to flee north.

Frederick Douglass was the alias of Frederick Augustus Washington Bailey, a young slave in Tuckahoe, Maryland. Bailey had been born in 1817 to a white man and a black slave, Harriet Bailey. Escaping in 1838, the youth made his way first to New York City and then to New Bedford, Massachusetts.

The twenty-one-year-old fugitive hoped to find work in the demanding but lucrative trade of boat caulker. However, white tradesmen in New Bedford refused to let blacks work as caulkers, or to practice any highly paid manual skill that required an apprenticeship for training. Like many blacks in New Bedford, Bailey worked as a laborer.

During that period Bailey changed his last name to Douglass, partly to conceal his identity from kidnappers and partly out of gratitude to a Quaker named Douglass who had assisted his escape from Maryland. At the same time he started attending antislavery meetings and began subscribing to William Lloyd Garrison's newspaper *The Liberator*. Shortly thereafter, Douglass met Garrison, Wendell Phillips, and other leaders in the Massachusetts Anti-Slavery Society. The white abolitionists were so impressed with Douglass that in 1841 they appointed him agent and lecturer for the society. He never worked as a laborer again. In his new job he solicited members for the society and sold subscriptions to the *National Anti-Slavery Standard* and *The Liberator*. Many white abolitionists, who solicited members and sold subscriptions were not so fortunate as Douglass, and suffered death and injury along with blacks at the hands of angry white immigrants and white southerners.

In 1845, Douglass fully entered public life with the publication of his autobiography, *Narrative of the Life of Frederick Douglass, An American Slave*. His book became a bestseller, but the publicity also exposed Douglass—still a fugitive—to possible recapture. When antislavery forces in England invited him to lecture and promote his book, he accepted the offer right away. During his two years in England, Douglass spoke at rallies and wrote for the antislavery cause.

When he returned to America, he decided to publish a paper to promote his appeals. However, Douglass did not want to compete with *The Liberator*, *The Anti-Slavery Standard*, and other white abolitionist papers located in New York City or Boston, so he chose to publish his paper in Rochester, New York.

THE NORTH STAR

The final issues of *The Ram's Horn* had carried ads for a new antislavery newspaper from Rochester, New York, *The North Star*, published and edited by Frederick Douglass. The first issue appeared November 1, 1847. *The North Star's* masthead proclaimed, "Right is of no Sex—Truth is of no Color—God is the Father of us all, and we are all Brethren."

Promising to be "mainly Anti-Slavery," a "terror to evil doers," *The North Star* stated that it would cover "all measures and topics of a moral and humane character, which may serve to enlighten, improve and elevate mankind."[1] The paper had four eighteen by twenty-six inch pages of seven columns each with small boldface headings. Readers of *The North Star* could depend on finding abolitionist propaganda such as the Reverend Henry Ward Beecher's speeches on "Abolition of Slavery in New England," addresses of Lucretia Mott, and speeches of Douglass—the usual abolitionist emphasis on opinions rather than news. However, *The North Star* featured prominently the brutality of slavery and marked a new kind of black journalism. The following item was typical:

Wm. A. Andrews, an overseer of J. W. Perkins, Mississippi, attempted to chastise one of the negro boys who seized a stick and prepared to do battle. The overseer told the boy to lay the

stick down or he would shoot him; he refused,
and the overseer then fired his pistol, and shot
the boy in the face, killing him instantly. The
jury of inquest found the verdict, "that the said
Wm. A. Andrews committed the killing in self-
defense."[2]

Douglass's editorials in *The North Star* were confrontational in style, militant in tone, and in the eyes of some of Douglass's readers, too rigid.

On the whole, Douglass was not so much more radical than other abolitionists. He was, to be sure, among the most eloquent and well known. Depending on one's politics, one considered him either the most admirable or the most infuriating abolitionist. While editor of *The North Star*, Douglass was subject to harassment and threats. His house was burned and twelve volumes of his newspaper were destroyed. On the streets of Rochester he met open hostility and abuse. *The New York Herald* declared, "The editor [Douglass] should be exiled to Canada and his presses thrown into the lake."[3]

But the most serious problem for *The North Star* was financial. Douglass was strapped by the costs of *The North Star*, in spite of sizable start-up capital he had received from English abolitionists. On May 5, 1848, *The North Star* printed an urgent appeal to its subscribers for money to continue operations. Similar appeals followed, but they all failed to bring in enough donations to balance the books. The paper was about to fold.

Mrs. Julia Griffiths Crofts, an English friend of Douglass's, responded to the paper's emergency. She relieved him of management of the paper while he raised money to pay bills. A few months later, however, the increasing costs of *The North Star* forced

Douglass to mortgage his home. Afterward, the paper's level of support declined. Publishing for a circulation of three thousand cost eighty dollars a week and increasingly required financing that Douglass lacked.

Douglass no longer controlled the business and editorial policies of the paper. In June 1851, there was talk of a merger with the Liberty party paper, a weekly with fewer than seven hundred subscribers, edited and published by John Thomas in Syracuse and financed by white abolitionist Gerrit Smith. The merger seemed to make sound business sense as an expansion of the paper's sales volume. The free black population, which had increased to a half million, was divided between 230,000 persons in the slave states and 260,000 in the free states. The market seemed enormously promising. But Douglass now had to share decisions with John Thomas, his editorial assistant; Julia Griffiths Crofts, the business manager; and Gerrit Smith, the paper's banker. Debts mounted, Douglass and his partners quarreled, and expenses each week exceeded revenues by as much as thirty dollars, a large loss at the time for a small business.

THE ROAD TO WAR

As the fortunes of Douglass's paper turned worse, the prospects for ending slavery improved. In the late 1840s and 1850s, abolitionists, under the prodding of men like Douglass, had become more politically organized and more sympathetic to militant agitation. The largely inept Liberty party had been reorganized in 1848 as the Free Soil party, and for the first time, a national convention of blacks had appealed for black political unity to fight legal discrimination.

By 1850, membership in abolitionist and anti-slavery societies in northern states had reached 150,000. With an increase in sympathetic white readers, black newspapers seemed to spring up everywhere. The country was sliding into civil war, and there was no turning back.

Kentucky Senator Henry Clay's Compromise of 1850, which the Congress passed, provoked antislavery forces to redouble their campaign. Called a "final solution" to the issue, Clay's Compromise had a strong fugitive slave provision, mandating six months' imprisonment and a fine of one thousand dollars for anyone caught aiding a fugitive. The Compromise abolished slavery in the District of Columbia, strengthened the Fugitive Slave Act, and admitted New Mexico, California, and Utah as free territories. Northerners were enraged that runaways could be apprehended in the North and returned to southern bondage. Douglass declared: "Some men go for the abolition of slavery by peaceful means. So do I, I am a peace man, but I recognize in the Southern States at the moment . . . a state of war."[4]

Contrary to expectations, the Compromise intensified the antislavery debate, for neither side would accept a partial victory. Responses by abolitionists to the Fugitive Slave Law were almost uniformly defiant.

Abby Kelley, a leader of the Quakers, known as the Society of Friends, echoed Douglass's views. Going a logical step further, Kelley stated: "The question is not whether we shall counsel the slaves to foresake peace, and commence war; *the war exists already* and has been waged unremittingly ever since the slave has been in bondage."[5]

Boston's Lewis Hayden, an escaped slave himself, hid fugitives in his house and publicly let it be known that his house was booby-trapped with dynamite.

Martin R. Delany avowed, "If any man approaches [my] house in search of a slave . . . [or] crosses the threshold of my door, and I do not lay him a lifeless corpse at my feet, I hope the grave may refuse my body a resting place, and righteous Heaven my spirit a home."[6] And Wendell Phillips, not to be outdone in rhetoric, told a Boston crowd, "Law or no law, Constitution or no Constitution, humanity shall be paramount."[7]

"If we are abolitionists," argued Horace Mann in an address in the winter of 1850, "then we are abolitionists of human bondage."[8] Abolitionists exposed undercover slave catchers in stores, trolleys, and other public places. Mobs helped fugitive defendants escape courthouse cells during proceedings, and the recapture of escapees, as one congressional committee reported, led to "unpleasant, if not perilous collisions."[9]

The other side was not slow to react. Newly elected President Millard Fillmore (1850–1853) condemned abolitionists as "lawless and violent mobs."[10] John C. Calhoun, in his farewell address to the Senate, March 4, 1850, eloquently described the dangerous collision course on which the nation was headed. Directing his words to the North, Calhoun wrote:

The agitation has been permitted to proceed, with almost no attempt to resist it, until it has reached a period when it can no longer be disguised or denied that the Union is in danger. . . . If something decisive is not done to arrest it, the South will be forced to choose between abolition and secession. . . .[11]

The stage was set in the North for massive protests against racial discrimination. One of the first demonstrations came from the Reverend James W. C. Pennington, an escaped slave and former blacksmith in New York City.

Pennington wrote the first black history; read Greek, German, and Latin; and obtained a doctor of divinity degree from the University of Heidelberg. In 1850, "Dr. P.," as he was called, refused to ride on the racially segregated front platform of the Sixth Avenue horse-drawn trolley. Although the trolley conductor physically ejected him from the car, his protest sparked copy-cat sit-ins, front-page headlines in the press, and the largest civil rights demonstrations up to that time in New York City.

Now a new force emerged, the Republican party, which in 1850 caused a number of northern states to enact personal liberty laws to protect free blacks from reenslavement. Emerging from the Free Soil party, the Republican party was well organized and well financed by an old-monied class of northern merchants, farmers, craftspeople, bankers, clergy, educators, and industrialists and was utterly committed to immediate and full emancipation of the slaves. The party constituted the first serious political and military threat to the southern slaveholders since British warships tried to induce slave rebellions off the Carolina coasts in 1815. The Republicans turned a blind eye, or winked, when fifty fugitives declared at a convention in Cazenovia, New York, that slaves had the right "to plunder, burn and kill" to escape.[12] In the spring of 1851, thanks to Republican pressure, Maine prohibited reenslavement.

Meanwhile, Douglass's paper came to an end. In 1851, the title of *The North Star* was changed to *Frederick Douglass' Paper*, with Douglass as editor. Although the paper supposedly continued his policies, it no longer ran "F.D." at the bottom of his articles. Douglass's newspaper finally suspended publication in 1864.

By the time the paper collapsed, however, it had raised the professional standards for the newer abolitionist newspapers. Its coverage and readership, moreover, had extended all over the United States, Canada, Europe, and the West Indies. Indeed the only black periodical of political importance just before the Civil War was *The North Star*.

During this time free blacks had created an extensive record of their lives in dozens of autobiographies, thirty-two newspapers, thousands of recorded speeches, sermons, pamphlets, nine magazines, published and unpublished poems, dramas, novels, plays, and short tales. The founders of the black press, Russwurm and Cornish, were long gone. But a decisive battle with slavery, the purpose of *Freedom's Journal*, was imminent.

Writes historian Lerone Bennett, Jr.:

The militant phase of the anti-slavery movement was inaugurated by black pioneers, who did more to help themselves than their more celebrated allies. Of at least equal consequence is the fact that blacks were instrumental in focusing the demands of the new movement. Most of the pioneer white abolitionists were in the orbit of innocuous and sentimental paternalism until they were educated and transformed by the black pioneers. It is established beyond doubt, for instance, that Samuel E. Cornish and other black leaders were primarily responsible for turning William Lloyd Garrison against the deportation ideas of the American Colonization Society.[13]

V

ADVOCATES AND ABOLITIONISTS

FUGITIVE SLAVES RESPOND TO ABOLITIONIST MESSAGE

The Kansas-Nebraska Act of 1854, sponsored by Senator Stephen A. Douglas, strengthened the Fugitive Slave laws and allowed settlers in the western territories to decide whether their new states would enter the Union as slave or free states. As a result, armed settlers from both regions poured into the territory to fix—by intimidation and electoral fraud—the state's status. In one celebrated case, slaveholders trying to auction a boy at Iowa Point in the territory were attacked and killed by Free-Soilers who rescued the boy. Southerners in response cursed that every northerner was an abolitionist and "every white-livered abolitionist who dares to set foot in Kansas (territory) should be hung."[1]

In the far north, slave catchers were seldom a threat. In any case they would have probably found it unpleasant to visit Grand Rapids, Michigan. The town in 1855 formed a military company of volunteers for the express purpose of protecting runaways; the militia's slogan was "Northern rights and Northern men."[2] Farther south, Texans had to form militias to recapture slaves fleeing into Mexico with the help of Mexican officials. So the positions hardened and each side became more menacing.

In the border states, free blacks and slave catchers increasingly clashed. On September 15, 1851, Mr. Gorsuch, a white slaveholder, led a United States marshall and a posse of twenty men into Christiana, Pennsylvania, in search of two of Gorsuch's slaves. The posse was met by the Negro Vigilance Committee of William Parker, who was hiding the runaways, Samuel Thompson and another unidentified man. When the whites entered Parker's house and attempted to climb the stairs to the second floor, they encountered Parker and members of the committee, rifles at the ready, standing above them barring the way. Heated words passed between the men; in a flash, Thompson struck Gorsuch and the white men began to fire, wounding two men. According to Parker, "At this time all the white men opened fire, and we rushed upon them; when they turned, threw down their guns, and ran away. We, being closely engaged, clubbed our rifles. We were too closely pressed to fire, but we found a good deal could be done with empty guns. . . . When the white men ran, they scattered."[3] The posse was no match for the committee. After the riot was over, Gorsuch was dead and his son and his nephew badly wounded. The fugitives were never recaptured.

Certainly, living in the North, rather than fleeing into Canada, was a hazard for fugitives. Anthony Burns, a Virginian fugitive, was recaptured in Boston, causing an uprising that had to be suppressed by twenty-two units of marines, cavalry, and artillery,

as thousands of Bostonians tried to protect him. A
fiery white radical, John Brown, noted then that the
fugitive slave laws were creating "more abolitionists
than all the lectures" and propaganda.[4] Boston, after
all, was the same city that twenty years earlier
had chased William Lloyd Garrison out of town. A
change had occurred in public attitudes. Boston had
become an abolitionist town, unsafe for slave
catchers.

WOMEN AS ABOLITIONISTS

One of the key developments in abolitionist strategy
was to link the antislavery cause with feminist aspirations. At a women's rights convention attended by
Elizabeth Cady Stanton and Susan B. Anthony in
New York City, May 1851, male speakers had
bluntly told the predominantly female audience that
women were biologically, mentally, and emotionally
inferior to men, hence natural second-class citizens.
From the rear of the hall, a tall black woman strode
to the platform, unannounced and unbeckoned by
the male speaker. Pushing herself in front of the last
man to speak, Sojourner Truth stood in front of the
podium. "Dat little man in black dar," she said in
dialect, "he say women can't have as much rights as
men, 'cause Christ wasn't a woman! Whar did your
Christ come from? From God and a woman! Man has
nothin' to do wid Him."[5] The audience broke into
thunderous applause; Truth, an illiterate former
New York slave, stirred her audience and immediately became a heroine to the women's rights
movement. Women were natural allies of the slaves.
Truth lived up to her role. She led protests against
segregation in northern cities, and though she was

illiterate, she skillfully debated educated male opponents on slavery and women's rights.

In the contest for white sympathy, two publications assisted the antislavery cause. One had been Harriet Beecher Stowe's novel, *Uncle Tom's Cabin*, depicting in starkly graphic scenes the cruelties of slavery inflicted on mostly angelic black and mixed-race slaves. Although Stowe's novel had been serialized the previous year in *National Era*, the hardcover novel published in 1852 sold over three hundred thousand copies in the first year. One southern literary critic challenged the book's authenticity and denounced it as "criminal prostitution on the high function of the imagination."[6] A free black in Maryland was sentenced to ten years in prison for owning a copy.

Another sensational best-selling novel had appeared in 1852, *Clotel, or the President's Daughter*, featuring a remarkable black woman character. The novel was authored by a former runaway, William Wells Brown, who had become a liberator of slaves. Brown, a storywriter, actor, and dramatist, had taught himself to read and write and, unlike many former slaves, disdained religion. "My religion," he often said, "was to help do away with the curse of American slavery."[7]

In November 1853, a controversial court case involved black education. Virginia, like other southern states, had laws forbidding the education of free blacks by any white person, unless the education was of a religious nature and counseled blacks to obey whites. Mrs. Margaret Douglass, a white teacher, was arrested in Norfolk, Virginia, for teaching free black children how to read and write. She was tried and convicted before the circuit court, and although the jury fined her only one dollar, the prosecution sought and was granted a stiffer sentence. But Mrs. Douglass served only one month of a six month sentence in prison. Judge Richard Baker overturned her conviction January 10, 1854, in a major legal victory for free blacks.

The most important voice for free black emigration was that of a Canadian free woman, Mary Ann Shadd (later Mrs. Mary Ann Shadd Carey [1823–1893]), daughter of a black abolitionist leader from Wilmington, Delaware. Mary Ann was publisher and editor of *The Provincial Freeman* in Toronto and Chatham, Ontario, from 1854 to 1858. Active in the Underground Railroad and abolitionist efforts in the United States, she advocated emigration of free blacks to Canada, arguing that African Americans' progress would never match that of Canadian blacks.

Another famous writer of the times, Charlotte Forten, the daughter of black abolitionist Robert Forten, wrote a widely read essay published in 1854, "The Difficulty of Being A Negro Christian," which dealt with the barbarity of white imposed slavery on blacks. "I wonder," writes Charlotte Forten, "that every colored person is not a misanthrope. Surely we have everything to make us hate mankind. . . . [But] Conscience answers it is wrong, it is ignoble to despair."[8] Charlotte was not alone in her sentiments. Black publisher Martin R. Delany argued that American white men were unfit to "spread the Gospel as missionaries among the colored races."[9] In the words of Ralph Waldo Emerson, slavery's laws, ironically, were enforced by "people who could read and write."[10] In fact, sociologist George Fitzhugh, a southern intellectual who read and wrote very well, actually argued that slavery was a superior economic system to northern capitalism.

THE WESTERN FRONT

The several thousand blacks who moved westward found the West to be far more congenial than other parts of the country. Were it not for the difficulty of traveling west, blacks would have emigrated in greater numbers. But life beyond the Mississippi was dangerous and hard for anyone. The fewer black communities in the West meant fewer readers of black newspapers, yet the cause of antislavery did not wait for readers and financial success. Judge Mifflin W. Gibbs published the first black newspaper in the Far West, *The Mirror of the Times* (1855). The western publisher used his freedom, his fortune, and his influence to help fellow blacks still enslaved.

THE SOUTH

Surprisingly, not all the South was hostile to black freedom. Pockets of racial tolerance existed in urban seaports like Savannah, Georgia, and New Orleans, Louisiana. Whether because of the influx of large numbers of immigrants or because of less rigid Catholic and Latin racial attitudes, a large population of free blacks existed in New Orleans before the Civil War. The first newspapers published by black southerners appeared in June 1856, *The Semi-Weekly* and *Daily Creole* (later *The New Orleans Daily Creole*) published by Harmon, Latham and Co.

STORM CLOUDS

Events of the 1850s were not auspicious for peace nor for union. When in 1856 Charles Sumner, a Republican senator from Massachusetts, was attacked and physically beaten by Congressman Preston Brooks of South Carolina, one Virginia paper commended Brooks and urged others to assault all abolitionists.

In 1855, a Republican congressman, Abraham Lincoln, asked, "Can we as a nation continue permanently—forever—half slave and half free?"[11] The Republicans entered national politics in the 1856 presidential election to answer "No" and ran John C. Fremont as their first candidate. But Fremont's defeat weakened abolitionist hopes of ending slavery without violence. White radical John Brown of Lawrence, Kansas, also had a ready answer to Lincoln's question. Brown was an extremist prepared not only to kill but to die for the cause of antislavery: "I will die fighting."[12] Brown began to plot with his sons and a Scotsman, James Redpath, to instigate violent conflict between slaves and masters, and between North and South.

DRED SCOTT DECISION

Of all the preceding events, none was to further Brown's aim as much as the Supreme Court's Dred Scott Decision of 1857. Proslavery groups were ecstatic. The decision handed down by Chief Justice Roger Taney, a Maryland slaveholder and the first Roman Catholic chief justice, implied that all antislavery laws were unconstitutional; that blacks could never be full citizens, nor have the same civil rights as whites. Blacks, in Taney's words, had "no rights which the white man was bound to respect."[13] The decision seemed to open the new territory to slavery. Dred Scott, the black who brought the suit, was a fugitive who had lived in free states for four years. Taney's court had intended to deny Scott's petition to become a freeman but ironically, Scott's freedom was unaffected by the decision. Scott's master, a convert to the antislavery cause, had secretly arranged for him to petition the court, in the hope of overthrowing slavery. Two weeks after Scott's appeal was refused, his master manumitted him.

Predictably blacks in the North reacted with fury. But Frederick Douglass, addressing a New York meeting, declared on the day of the decision, "My hopes are never brighter than now."[14] Douglass noted that Taney's decision, like the Missouri Compromise and the Compromise of 1850, did not lead to resolution of the conflict, but rather moved the country closer to war—an abolitionist aim. Wryly, Douglass said, "The fact is, the more the question has been settled, the more it has needed settling."[15]

Robert Purvis and Charles L. Remond drew up a resolution that was read before a Philadelphia church. The resolution denounced the court, declaring that there could be "no allegiance due from any man, or any class of men, to a government founded and administered in iniquity. . . . Our hope is that . . . our white fellow slaves . . . will make common cause with us . . . and . . . join with us."[16]

Delegates to a black convention in Ohio resolved to study military tactics and to become more skilled with weapons. A biracial convention in Cleveland, attended by white feminists Susan B. Anthony and Elizabeth Cady Stanton and abolitionists Charles L. Remond and Parker Pillsbury, affirmed, "It is the duty of the slave to strike down their tyrant masters by force and arms wherever the blow, however bloody, can be made effective to that end . . . [and] whenever we behold them in the battlefield of freedom, we will give them every aid and comfort in our power."[17] Wendell Phillips in Boston endorsed violence in chilling terms, "If a Negro kills his master tonight, . . . say that he is a William Tell in disguise. . . . I want to accustom Massachusetts to the idea of insurrection, to the idea that every slave has a right to seize his liberty on the spot."[18] In New Orleans, however, repression intensified against black papers. Unable to overcome both white sabotage and poor sales, the New Orleans papers ceased publication in 1857.

In 1859, the year Samuel Cornish died, rebellion and conspiracy appeared spontaneously. A Boston lawyer, Lysander Spooner, published in the *Boston Courier* newspaper a military plan to free the slaves. Independently of Spooner, John Brown and a band of black and white raiders attacked Harper's Ferry, Virginia, on October 16, 1859, hoping to spark a slave uprising. On the very same day, Harriet Tubman, a runaway slave, was raiding plantations to lead slaves to freedom. Brown did not have Tubman's luck; for his troubles, he was captured and hanged, but in death, he became a martyr to the abolitionists.

Martin R. Delany, who in 1854 had inspired a black separatist mood by coining the phrase "Africa for the Africans,"[19] began the serialization of his novel, *Blake; or, The Huts of America*, which had as its main theme slave rebellion and one slave character who states, "I am for War—War upon the whites."[20]

In the 1860 presidential election Abraham Lincoln and the Republicans triumphed over proslavery candidate Stephen A. Douglas, a victory that greatly alarmed not only slaveholders but many whites who hoped to avoid a break-up of the country into hostile camps.

Immediately after Abraham Lincoln took the oath of office as president, the Democratic party split into northern and southern wings and South Carolina seceded from the Union. The war had begun, much to the satisfaction of both sides in the debate. A belligerent spirit filled the country. Everywhere, it seemed, people innocently unaware of the suffering to come would settle for nothing less than war.

VI

CIVIL WAR AND EMANCIPATION

On April 12, 1861, a young rebel commander, Pierre Beauregard, gave the order to fire on Fort Sumter, South Carolina, and to continue until loyal Union troops surrendered. The fort capitulated almost immediately to Beauregard, who later became a decorated Confederate general. From a Confederate point of view, slavery had been defended, but few people realized the potential of the conflict as well as black publishers did.

The *Anglo-American* newspaper, for instance, welcomed the southern secession and put forth the black view:

> No adjustment of the nation's difficulty is possible until the claims of the black man are first met and satisfied. . . . His prostrate body forms an impediment over which liberty cannot advance. . . . His title to life, to liberty, and

the pursuit of happiness must be acknowl-
edged, or the nation will be forsworn; and
being so, incur the dreadful penalty of perma-
nent disunion, unending anarchy, and perpet-
ual strife. . . .[1]

Frederick Douglass heard the news the next morning while out for a walk in New York City. He broke
into a cheer: "God be praised!"[2] But the war, which
had erupted with the shelling and surrender of Fort
Sumter, suspended nearly all publications of the
black press.

Wendell Phillips summed up the antislavery
strategy of promoting the conflict: "I never did believe in the capacity of Abraham Lincoln, but I do
believe in the pride of [Jefferson] Davis, in the vanity
of the South, in the desperate determination of those
fourteen states; and I believe in a sunny future, because God has driven them mad, and in their mad-
ness is our hope. . . ."[3]

President Lincoln issued a call for seventy-five
thousand volunteers, but the recruiting offices
turned away blacks who wanted to serve their country. Among the 115 black students from Wilberforce
University, Ohio, crowding an enlistment office, was
Richard Cain. He was told by the white officer in
charge "that this," in Cain's words, "was a white
man's war and that the Negro has nothing to do with
it."[4] Black veteran scout Jacob Dodson, who had accompanied Kit Carson and John Frémont on explora-
tions of the Pacific and Southwest, was also rejected
for service by Secretary of War Simon Cameron.

Racial issues were present in the war from the
very beginning, but Union war aims initially
avoided making abolition a war goal, much to the
dismay of abolitionists.

Abolitionist Governor John A. Andrews of Massachusetts, on learning of the Union Army ban on black troops, declared:

> *Every race has fought for liberty and its own progress. If Southern slavery should fall by the crushing of the Rebellion, and colored men should have no hand and play no conspicuous part in the task, the result would leave the colored man a mere helot.*[5]

Though he would not act on his convictions for political reasons, President Lincoln recognized early that black troops would give the Union a military advantage in the war. He expressed as much in a letter of March 24, 1861, to Tennessee Senator Andrew Johnson: "The bare sight of fifty thousand armed, and drilled black soldiers on the banks of the Mississippi would end the rebellion at once."[6] Lincoln's policy was adopted prematurely by Union generals John Frémont and Benjamin Butler. Whenever the Union generals liberated slaves, however, their orders were countermanded by Lincoln, who feared offending his slaveholding allies.

Still, Lincoln's earliest correspondence and political speeches show that he detested slavery, although he seemed genuinely perplexed by how to overcome racism. Finally on January 1, 1863, with the war at a stalemate, President Lincoln issued his Emancipation Proclamation freeing all slaves "forever free" in the Confederacy.[7]

The Union needed every ablebodied man available and willing to fight. Union military defeats had swayed public opinion in favor of mustering black troops. "All our increased military strength," remarked Naval Secretary Gideon Welles, "now comes from the negroes."[8] In March 1863, the War Department established the Bureau of Colored Troops to supervise black regiments. An exuberant General Ulysses S. Grant commented, "By arming the negro we have added a powerful ally."[9] Of the 178,975 blacks who served in the Union Army, 99,337 were from the slaveholding states.

In the summer of 1863, the first National Draft Act was passed, this time including blacks. Irish and other white ethnic immigrants rioted in New York City and Detroit to protest being drafted to serve in the military. White mobs in the New York draft riots killed many blacks and set a black orphanage on fire. Nevertheless, the war marked advances in black demands for equality. Illinois and California rushed through legislation ending discriminatory "Black Laws." Congress voted to permit blacks to testify in federal cases and opened the postal service to black employment.

BLACK PAPERS DURING THE WAR

The Colored Citizen, called "the Soldier's Organ" because of its circulation among black Union troops, was the only black newspaper to last for the duration of the Civil War. Frederick Douglass had devoted his full attention to his other publication, *Douglass' Monthly*, until it suspended publication in the summer of 1863. Being then too old for active service, Douglass recruited black soldiers in the South for the Union Army. In his farewell to his readers he wrote:

I have lived to see the leading presses of the country, willing and ready to publish any ar-

gument of appeal in behalf of my race, I am able to make. So that while speaking and writing are still needful, the necessity for a special organ for my views and opinions on slavery no longer exists. To this extent at least, my paper has accomplished the object of its existence. It had done something towards battering down that dark and frowning wall of partition between the working minds of two races, hitherto thought impregnable.[10]

Douglass had given forty years to the antislavery cause and he had been bankrupted by the effort. Yet he insisted that he was "more a debtor [to the cause of antislavery] than [the cause] is a debtor to me."[11]

When southern Louisiana was liberated in 1863, Lincoln authorized General Nathaniel P. Banks to offer the state's whites amnesty in return for loyalty to the Union. Banks continued a policy of using former slaves as paid workers on Louisiana's sugar cane plantations, which had been started by Banks's predecessor, General Benjamin F. Butler, who had punished former slaves who refused such work. Not only was black suffrage repugnant to Banks, but he extended the forced labor policy throughout postwar Louisiana.

Before the free black newspaper in New Orleans, *L'Union*, had folded in 1864, it had demanded suffrage for blacks. Now the cause was taken up by *The New Orleans Tribune*, founded by a mixed-race black, Louis C. Roudanez, and edited by an émigré, Belgian aristocrat Jean Charles Houzeau. *The Tribune* led the quest of New Orleans's free blacks to compel congressional action on behalf of freed slaves. *The Tribune* and *L'Union* condemned the Banks labor system as a reinstitution of slavery. Houzeau dedicated himself to Louisiana blacks, who were, he declared "the vanguard of the African population of the United States."[12] Under his editorship the paper denounced Banks for instituting a system that "chained" blacks to the soil and left them exposed to absentee northern plantation owners, "Banks's oligarchy." "Every man," *The Tribune* declared, "should own the land he tills."[13]

Houzeau wrote monthly editorials in *The Tribune* promoting black suffrage, legal equality, desegregation of Louisiana's schools and streetcars, and black ownership of plantation lands. His editorials were quoted in Europe as well as in the North. French novelist Victor Hugo sent him an approving letter. But Houzeau's greatest concern was to unite the light-skinned free "creole" blacks with darker-skinned blacks.

As he put it in one editorial:

These two populations, equally rejected and deprived of their rights, cannot be well estranged from one another. The emancipated will find, in the old freemen, friends ready to guide them, to . . . teach them their duties as well as their rights. . . . The freemen will find in the recently liberated slaves a mass to uphold them and with this mass behind them they will command the respect always bestowed to number and strength. . . .[14]

WHAT RECONSTRUCTION DID TO THE FREEDMEN

Confederate General Robert E. Lee's surrender to General Grant on April 9, 1865, brought the war to a close. The end of the Confederacy, however, produced new challenges to blacks. Few people realized both the promise and the danger of Emancipation as did black publishers. Frederick Douglass observed that blacks were free only to face hardships, such as the anger of the defeated white Confederates, and free to starve, freeze, and suffer the deprivations of disease and crime among themselves. Abolitionist Wendell Phillips remarked that the Emancipation Proclamation freed the slave, but ignored "the negro."[15]

After the end of the war, Democratic party women had paraded with banners saying "Fathers, save us from nigger husbands" and "The Union As It Is, The Constitution As It Was."[16] *The Cincinnati Enquirer* newspaper had written: "Slavery is dead, the negro is not. There is the misfortune."[17] The doctrine that the Supreme Court had declared in the case of fugitive slave Dred Scott (1857), that a black had no legal rights a white person need respect, still prevailed among the majority of whites.

With the war's end, abolitionists like Wendell Phillips insisted that Reconstruction could never be complete until blacks obtained full citizenship rights, including access to public education, ownership of land, and the ballot. To the radicals in the Republican party, Lincoln's Proclamation of Amnesty to the defeated South left blacks unprotected before their former masters.

Louisiana, as one of the first states to apply for readmission to the Union, set the stage for a consideration of black rights and new legislation. At the first Equal Rights League convention in New Orleans, in January 1865, *The Tribune*, which regarded all black and "colored" men as fellow sufferers, witnessed a new black unity. In the hall, the editor wrote, "There were seated side by side the rich and the poor, the literate and educated man and the country laborer hardly released from bondage

Frederick Douglass, an escaped slave who became
a leader of the antislavery movement, founded
and edited the newspaper *The North Star*.

In 1839, Africans who had been
kidnapped to be sold as slaves,
mutinied aboard the slave ship
Amistad off the coast of Cuba.
A slave revolt was the great
fear of slave owners. The
black newspapers were denounced
because their editors praised
the mutiny on the *Amistad*.
This mural painting is by
Hale Woodruff.

Below: Black Union soldiers
in the Civil War

Sojourner Truth, a former slave and a leader of the antislavery movement, was also a leader in the movement for women's right to vote.

Abraham Lincoln reads to his cabinet his Emancipation Proclamation freeing all slaves in the Confederacy. Emancipation was the goal of the black press until the Civil War.

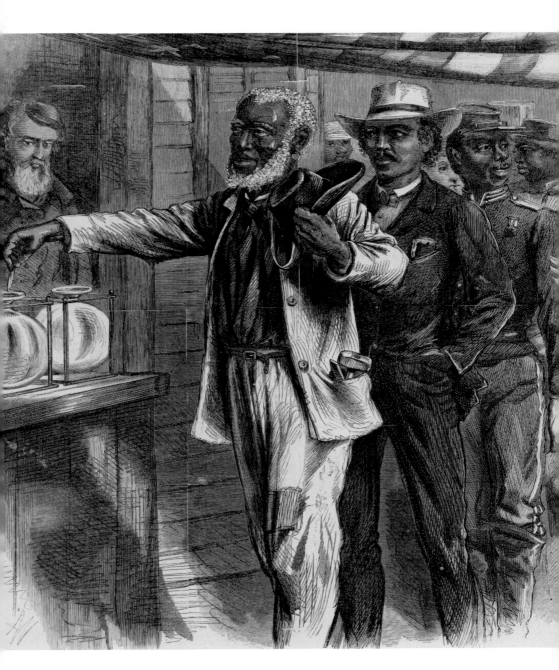

This 1867 drawing, which was popular in
the North, is entitled "The First Vote." The
Fourteenth Amendment to the Constitution
gave former male slaves the right to vote.

T. Thomas Fortune,
editor and publisher

An all-black army cavalry unit
assigned to the western frontier

The Ku Klux Klan was formed during
the period of Reconstruction to keep black
people from holding positions of power.
Members of the Klan used terror to
achieve this end, murdering black men who
dared to assert their new rights as citizens.

. . . the new champions of their race."[18] *The Tribune* won most of the state's blacks to a position of "self-help."[19] Because of the continued disenfranchisement of blacks and protests of *The Tribune*'s black and white supporters, Congress had refused to recognize Louisiana's electoral vote in the 1864 election.

The last black newspaper to be started before ratification of the Thirteenth Amendment freeing all slaves in the nation was *The Colored American* of Augusta, Georgia. Appearing in October 1865, the paper's first editorial bravely stated its resolve, in anticipation of new freedoms stemming from the Thirteenth Amendment, "to keep before the minds of our race the duties and responsibilities of freedom; and to call attention to the wants and grievances of the colored people."[20] *The American*, however, went into bankruptcy six months later. Black papers like the *Tribune* eloquently applauded the new amendment, while the *National Anti-Slavery Standard* immediately upped the ante of black freedom with a new motto on its masthead: "No Reconstruction Without Negro Suffrage."[21]

In 1865, Democrats in New Bedford, Massachusetts, ran a black for the state legislature. In general, the black vote was sought by Republicans and Democrats alike. The Republicans even nominated two black candidates for judgeships in 1866. Congress created the Freedmen's Bureau (1865–69) and passed the first Civil Rights Act (1866) giving blacks legal rights equal to those of whites, in an effort to nullify the postwar Black Codes that had been enacted by southern legislatures to prevent blacks from competing with whites. Congress also passed a Reconstruction Act extending voting privileges to blacks (1867) and in 1868 passed the Fourteenth Amendment protecting the civil rights of blacks from state interference. Radical Republicans, so called because they wanted to give blacks full equality immediately, had proposed the grand plan called Reconstruction, and ever since 1867 blacks had appeared ready to fully participate in the governments of the southern states. For the *New York Independent*, a Radical Republican paper, the courting of the black vote by both parties indicated "A New Era in American Politics."[22]

The *Independent*, however, celebrated the new era too soon. President Andrew Johnson, who succeeded the assassinated Lincoln, rejected three blacks nominated by the Republicans for commissioner of the Freedmen's Bureau. Meanwhile the white South began a relentless campaign of violence to subjugate blacks. Gradually, southern Democrats regained control of state governments and removed black people from political participation.

VII

RECONSTRUCTION AND THE BLACK PRESS

"Keeping blacks in their place," as white former slaveholders expressed their prejudice, was frustrated by Union military rule after the Civil War. Yet "If the war had smashed the Southern world," as southern historian Howell Cobb wrote, "it had left the Southern mind and will—the mind and will arising from, corresponding to, and requiring this world—entirely unshaken."[1] Tragically, just as the former Confederates sought a return of white supremacy, blacks wanted to learn to protect themselves from racism.

A barely literate black, thanks to the Freedmen's Bureau schools established March 1865 for freed slaves, would have been able to read a few black newspapers in the South, such as the *Nationalist* in Mobile, Alabama, which protested the flying of the Confederate flag on national holidays and criticized blacks for fearing to fly the American flag. Southern black papers like the *Nationalist* were fiercely and racially proud, urging freedmen "to put away 'nigger' plays and songs" and adopt the "plays and amusements [of] . . . free men and women . . ." and "stand up like men on behalf of [their] rights."[2] Already, however, newly won black freedom was being challenged.

THE KU KLUX KLAN AND WHITE VIOLENCE

By 1866, former Confederates in Pulaski, Tennessee, had formed a secret organization, the Ku Klux Klan, whose purpose was to terrorize blacks to prevent them from challenging white supremacy. Republican leader Carl Schurz reported to President Andrew Johnson:

Some planters held back their former slaves on their plantations by brute force. Armed bands of white men patrolled the country roads to drive back the Negroes wandering about. Dead bodies of murdered Negroes were found on and near the highways and by-paths. Gruesome reports came from the hospitals—reports of colored men and women whose ears had been cut off, whose skulls had been broken by blows, whose bodies had been slashed by knives or lacerated by scourge.[3]

Former Confederates had little trouble handling former slaves. A pro-Union black *New Orleans Times* deplored the forced labor of freed slaves by former Confederate planters, vividly recounting the price blacks had to pay for resistance: "To see the Negroes mutilated and literally beaten to death as they sought to escape, was one of the most horrid pictures it has ever been our ill-fortune to witness."[4] And the *New Orleans Tribune*, one of the most professional of the black papers, angrily railed against the reversal of black freedom: "We were and still are oppressed; we are not demoralized criminals."[5]

The *Tribune* lost its federal and state printing contracts; its editor Houzeau emigrated to Jamaica and the paper folded in 1868. The Fourteenth Amendment, adopted in 1868, reaffirmed the rights granted by the Thirteenth Amendment and the Civil Rights Act of 1865. The amendment also guaranteed suffrage (although blacks were not explicitly mentioned).

The Thirteenth Amendment reflected Lincoln's desire to expand the Emancipation Proclamation's manumission of slaves. The proclamation, a wartime measure designed to weaken the Confederacy's economy and create social chaos, had freed only slaves living in the rebel states. In the campaign of 1864, Lincoln had led the effort of the Republicans to prohibit slavery wherever it existed. On January 31, 1865, three months before Lincoln's assassination, the measure passed as a constitutional amendment in both branches of Congress and was ratified by the states on December 18, 1865. The first section declared, "Neither slavery nor involuntary servitude, except as a punishment for crime, whereof the party shall have been duly convicted, shall exist within the United States, or any place subject to their jurisdiction."

The Civil Rights Act of 1866 bestowed citizenship rights on former slaves. The act attempted to suppress Black Codes of the former states of the Confederacy, which aimed to restore the ability of whites to deny civil rights to blacks. The act enabled blacks to bring suit against state laws that were discriminatory in federal court.

The Fourteenth Amendment to the Constitution, ratified by the states in 1868, declared that all persons, born or naturalized, were citizens and were protected from actions of states to abridge their privileges, such as voting. The amendment prohibited discrimination, such as the denial by a state or federal court of due process of law and equal protection under the law, and provided for penalties such as a proportional reduction of congressional representation for states that violated the amendment. Three other sections disqualified former legislators who rebelled against the Union from serving in federal office, rejected all compensation to slave owners for the purchase price and upkeep of slaves freed by the Thirteenth Amendment, and gave Congress power to enforce the provisions of the amendment.

The Fifteenth Amendment was ratified in 1870; it secured blacks the right to vote, establishing that "The right of citizens of the United States to vote shall not be denied or abridged by the United States or by any State on account of race, color, or previous condition of servitude."

White mobs led by former Confederates sought to deny blacks equal constitutional protection, either directly or indirectly through intimidation of local courts. Although the Civil Rights Acts and the Thirteenth, Fourteenth, and Fifteenth amendments provided for federal protection against state discrimination, cases of discrimination by private citizens and white mob violence against blacks posed a problem for the law. In one case, when several white men in Louisiana broke up an 1870s black political rally, the Supreme Court ruled against black plaintiffs, claiming that the Fourteenth Amendment's federal protection of blacks did not cover "private acts."6

In an effort to close the loophole in the amendments, Congress passed the Enforcement Acts of 1870 and 1871, requiring local governments to punish private violations of black civil rights. But without federal power, blacks were intimidated from exercising their legal rights. When the courts, the police, and the legislature were controlled by racist whites, and when the state turned its back on white gang violence against blacks, virtually all appeals for federal protection fell on deaf ears. The Fifteenth Amendment, for instance, had been ratified in 1870 and further protected the right to vote. Congress, however, undid each protection for blacks with a measure for the defeated Confederates, permitting whites to resume law enforcement and to control the courts.

Between 1870 and 1877, blacks slowly were stripped of all legal standing. In 1872 Congress passed the Amnesty Act, which made it possible for former Confederates to resume political activity. By then, blacks like Blanche K. Bruce had entered state politics, so that in South Carolina and Mississippi they formed a majority. Bruce became the first black Senator from Mississippi, the only black elected to the Senate for the next century. Although it seemed only fair to let the former Confederates once again participate in the political process, in fact the Amnesty Act signaled the return of white supremacy.

Whites like William Henderson and Senator Ben Tillman of South Carolina opposed fair elections. As Henderson put it,

We don't propose to have any fair elections. We will get left at that every time. [Laughter] Who

will be the managers? . . . I tell you, gentle-
men, if we have fair elections in Berkeley we
can't carry it. [Laughter] There's no use to talk
about it. The black man is learning to read
faster than the white man. And if he comes up
and can read you have got to let him vote.[7]

After a string of black lynchings in 1875, Congress
enacted another Civil Rights Act to guarantee blacks
equal rights in public accommodations. The Civil
Rights Act of 1875 would turn out to be not so much a
protection for blacks as a means for white Republicans to bully white southerners. The Hinds County
Mississippi Gazette proclaimed on September 29,
1875, "The people of this State are now fully armed,
equipped, and drilled. . . . "[8] Blacks who spoke out
against white violence were enrolled in "dead
books," marked for killing by whites. Race riots, in
which blacks were provoked into fighting against
superior numbers, started in county after county. In
Mississippi, in 1875, 150 blacks had lost their lives to
the mobs. For years to follow, black leaders in each
district across the state were systematically lynched.
When federal troops called inquests to capture the
whites, black witnesses were silenced by white as-
sassins. White terror spread to Memphis, Tennessee;
Charleston, South Carolina; and North Carolina,
Virginia, Texas, Alabama, and Georgia.
     In South Carolina Senator Wade Hampton orga-
nized a gang of whites known as Red Shirts. In 1876
they massacred a large group of blacks in Hamburg,
South Carolina. "White Men's Clubs" sprung up all
across the South as Democratic party clubs of each
county. *The Mississippi Columbus Democrat* stated
that the purpose of the clubs was to see "that white
men shall govern. . . . Nigger voting, holding office,

and sitting in the jury box, are all wrong, and against the sentiment of the country."[9]

The Forest, Mississippi, newspaper *Register* had on its masthead the slogan "A white man in a white man's place. A black man in a black man's place. Each according to the eternal fitness of things."[10] Other white newspapers in the state echoed the sentiment. The Yazoo *City Banner* warned, "Mississippi is a white man's country, and by the Eternal God we'll rule it."[11] *The Handsboro Democrat* called for "A white man's government, by white men, for the benefit of white men."[12]

In 1876 the Radical Republican government of South Carolina had been overthrown by conservative whites. State legislator Robert Aldrich had a literacy requirement enacted to disenfranchise blacks while reserving for illiterate whites the right to vote. A white movement for woman's suffrage, the South Carolina Equal Rights Association, tried unsuccessfully to convince white conservatives that giving white women the vote would strengthen white supremacy. Meanwhile Klan terror exploded. Blacks were afraid to sleep indoors at night for fear of midnight riders aiming to torch black homes. The victims often included pregnant women, children, the aged, the sick, as well as any black who taught school or who could be considered "uppity."

Senator Ben Tillman announced that when whites in South Carolina came to power, "We took the government away. We stuffed the ballot boxes. We shot Negroes! We are not ashamed of it."[13]

Simultaneously there were riots in Philadelphia, New York City, and Baltimore. South Carolina black Republican Robert Smalls estimated that fifty-three thousand blacks were killed by white violence during the Reconstruction period, and only three whites were convicted for the murders.

Prejudice in the Republican party undermined black political ambitions. Presidents Andrew Johnson and Ulysses S. Grant were openly sympathetic to an alliance with white southerners, who ignored the Civil Rights acts. With the election of the Republican Rutherford B. Hayes in 1876, blacks had lost army protection from white terror. Federal troops withdrew from South Carolina and Louisiana in 1877. White Democrats immediately acquired abandoned Union cannons and organized assassination squads. In a region of the country where there was a frontier code of justice, where disputes were settled outside the courtroom, thousands of young whites took part in racial violence.

Radical Republican power to protect blacks was limited to the enactment of laws, not their enforcement, nor their administration in disputes in the local and state courts. A political and constitutional definition of equality meant very little to blacks who were controlled by formerly Confederate bankers, merchants, and landlords, a white elite supported in turn by thousands of former army veterans willing to intimidate any black challengers. Of what good was the protection of the Fourteenth Amendment against the Black Code vagrancy statute of Alabama, which inflicted thirty-nine lashes on a black found to have no permanent address or work?

The popular image that whites held of blacks, the "Sambo" stereotype that blacks were lazy and simple creatures, almost monkeylike, had been greatly modified by the performance of black Union soldiers. Still, the experience of treating blacks as legal equals was a new one. There would be many difficulties ahead for the nation and the black press.

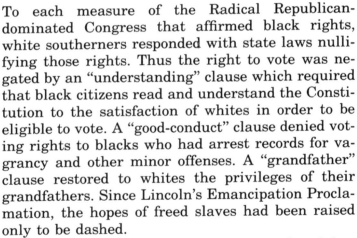

VIII

THE CRUSADER—
T. THOMAS FORTUNE

To each measure of the Radical Republican-dominated Congress that affirmed black rights, white southerners responded with state laws nullifying those rights. Thus the right to vote was negated by an "understanding" clause which required that black citizens read and understand the Constitution to the satisfaction of whites in order to be eligible to vote. A "good-conduct" clause denied voting rights to blacks who had arrest records for vagrancy and other minor offenses. A "grandfather" clause restored to whites the privileges of their grandfathers. Since Lincoln's Emancipation Proclamation, the hopes of freed slaves had been raised only to be dashed.

The new generation of publishers and activists had been very young at Emancipation or did not experience slavery at all. White racists would find this generation more militant and far more resourceful and cunning than the earlier publishers, such as Houzeau, Delany, and Garnet, whose voices had been stilled. One of the new publishers was T. Thomas Fortune.

T. THOMAS FORTUNE
(OCTOBER 3, 1856–JUNE 2, 1928)

In the 1870s white newspapers increasingly were using stereotypes in their portrayals of blacks. In this bleak social atmosphere a handsome black journalist, T. Thomas Fortune of New York, was beginning to find a national readership for his militant editorials denouncing racism. One edition of his New York City's *Globe* read: "There is no law in the United States for the Negro. The whole thing is a beggarly farce."[1] When a U.S. Supreme Court decision upheld segregation in Texas, Fortune's editorial declared: "The Supreme Court now declares that railroad corporations are free to force us into smoking cars or cattle cars; that hotel keepers are free to make us walk the streets at night, that theater managers can refuse us admittance. . . . We are aliens in our own land."[2]

One of the most distinguished and influential black journalists of his period, Fortune was the first-born son of mixed-race slave parents, Emanuel and Sarah Jane Fortune, who lived in Marianna, Florida. Fortune's grandfather had been an educated Irishman and his grandmother, a slave woman of Seminole, African, and white ancestry. The Irish Fortune had been killed in a duel by a white planter, according to Fortune, because the planter resented the Irishman's kindness to slaves. Only after Emancipation was the family permitted to adopt the Fortune name as its own.

Fortune first moved to Washington, D.C., where he worked on a black weekly, the *People's Advocate,* and attended law classes at night. In Washington, Fortune encountered segregation in public accommodations for the first time. Young Fortune had just arrived from Florida and taken a room in a hotel, but when the desk clerk discovered that the fair skinned youth was of black ancestry, he ejected Fortune from the hotel.

What most angered Fortune about the humiliation was that he experienced it in the North, for Florida and most of the deep South had not *yet* segregated public accommodations. When he returned to Florida, he discovered that his home state had become even more rigidly segregated than the North. The death of his first child in Jacksonville further discouraged him from settling in Florida.

THE *GLOBE*

Fortune moved to New York in 1881 and worked at a number of small white weeklies while in his spare time assisting a black weekly, *The Rumor*. Soon he became full-time editor of the paper and changed its name to the *Globe*. He quickly discovered that white news services refused to provide news to the paper. This discrimination, which might have defeated a less ambitious person, only goaded Fortune to develop a network of black reporters around the country. One of these reporters was a young schoolboy in Great Barrington, Massachusetts, W. E. B. DuBois, who was to become a leading black intellectual and a founder of the National Association for the Advancement of Colored People (NAACP).

Due to Fortune's experience as a copy editor and typographer, the *Globe* was remarkably free of grammatical and printing errors. Under Fortune's leadership, the weekly acquired a reputation for

exceptional news coverage, lucid writing, and provoca-
tive, courageous editorials. Two years after its founding
the *Globe* was being sold all over the country.

Editorials by Fortune attracted an audience
among both races. Unlike the moderate opinions in
many black papers, Fortune's writings called for mil-
itance, defiance, and independence. Typical of his
editorials was the *Globe*'s response to a Danville,
Virginia, race riot, which had started when a white
man was pushed by a black on a sidewalk. Many
black papers counseled blacks to defer to white
abuse, but Fortune wrote: "If it is necessary for colored men to turn themselves into outlaws to assert
their manhood and their citizenship, let them do it."[3]

The editor of the *Macon Telegram* in Georgia
accused Fortune of wanting social equality and intermarriage with whites. Fortune responded in the
Globe: "What every colored man wants . . . is the
concession of every right given to the white man
under the laws of the United States. . . . Call this
social equality if you will."[4]

Although Fortune detested white racism, he was
hardly uncritical of racist attitudes among blacks.
When Frederick Douglass married a white woman,
many blacks criticized his choice on grounds that it
betrayed the race. Fortune remembered that white
women had attacked white men like his grandfather
for consorting openly with black women. With a personal sense of irony, Fortune wrote that black objec-
tions to interracial marriages supported the white
racist claim "that the human nature of the black man
and the human nature of the white man differ in
some indefinable way, when we all know that, essen-
tially human nature is . . . the same wherever mankind is found."[5]

Because of his strong sense of independence, Fortune refused a Republican party subsidy in the 1880s

even though the *Globe* was deeply in debt. Fortune did not hesitate to criticize the Republican party when it refused to protect black voting rights and remained silent as white southerners imposed the Black Codes. At the time of the 1884 election, Fortune wrote an editorial supporting the Democratic candidate for president, Grover Cleveland. Other members of the paper's staff supported the Republican candidate, James G. Blaine. The division at the *Globe* made staff cooperation impossible and the paper folded.

Fortune then started his own newspaper, *The New York Freeman*, which continued his militant and independent style. The state of Georgia had removed state funds for black schools and deprived blacks of legal standing in the state courts. Declared the *Freeman*: "The white men of the South—in legislatures, in courts of justice, in convict camps, in churches, in hotels and theatres, in railroad and steamboat accommodations—do not do justice to their colored fellow citizens; and when a man (like Grady) stands up and lies about these matters, we are here to strike the lie in the head and we shall strike it."[6]

Fortune also supported Prohibition in the *Globe* and the *Freeman*, urging blacks to reject liquor and tobacco for "lemonade and ice cream."[7]

In 1887 Fortune turned over the management of the paper to his brother Emanuel who changed its name to the *New York Age*. Fortune continued to write for the *Age* (and also for the *New York Sun*), contributing to every section of the paper except the financial column. Two years later in 1889 his brother fell ill and died, and Fortune returned as editor of the paper.

After a brief spell of trying out the new life of freedom, blacks around the country felt a chilly political blast in the 1880s. In this dark and harsh period, white attitudes in the South were overwhelmingly hostile to any black advance. Twenty years after the end of the Civil War, free blacks had been reduced to what historian John Hope Franklin called a "quasi-freedom."[8]

In 1883, an audience at the Atlanta Opera House broke into "thunderous applause . . . as was never before heard within the walls of the opera house" when it was told that the Supreme Court had declared the 1875 Civil Rights Act unconstitutional.[9] Nothing stopped the efforts of former Confederates to deny blacks full civil rights. The number of lynchings of blacks rose yearly, reaching into the hundreds. Douglass, though alarmed, had refused to endorse black retaliation, fearing that untrained and disorganized former-slave military units could not defeat "trained armies, skilled generals of the Confederate army, and in the last resort . . . the Federal army."[10]

In 1889, Fortune returned to the Republican party, and again became editor of the *Age*. Fortune lived up to his reputation as "the Afro-American agitator." He promised that he would signal "the death knell of the shuffling, cringing creature in black who for two centuries and a half had given the right of way to white men. . . . "[11] He chastised the Democratic party for not interfering in the suppression of black political participation in the South. So biting were his editorials that young Theodore Roosevelt, the future president, was reputed to have told him in a meeting, "Tom Fortune, for God's sake, keep that pen of yours off me."[12]

Republican Representative Henry Cabot Lodge tried to have Congress pass a "Force Bill" protecting black rights but in 1890 the bill went down in defeat. As the situation worsened for blacks and the yearly number of lynchings claimed almost three hundred black victims, Fortune called for the creation of a civil rights organization to redress racist laws. In January 1890, 151 delegates from local organizations in twenty-one states met in Chicago to form the Afro-American League, but the delegates could not agree on a structure of leadership and the league collapsed. On returning to New York, Fortune entered a Manhattan hotel saloon and was refused service on grounds of race. He sued the hotel and received an award of $1,016. At least the league had one victory in its short life.

As the 1900s began, efforts to justify lynching appeared everywhere. White leaders like Senator Ben Tillman cultivated the image of blacks as beasts. According to Tillman, a black was "a fiend, a wild beast, seeking whom he may devour."[13] A popular essay, *The Negro, A Beast* written in 1900 by Charles Carroll, argued that blacks were apes and not really human.

In 1898, two years before Carroll's book appeared, Fortune had convened another civil rights council at Rochester, New York, to establish the Afro-American Council. The council divided on the degree to which it should support the Republican party. Fortune accused Republican President William McKinley of "glorifying rebellion, mobocracy, and the murder of [black] women and children."[14] Soon the council fell under the control of Booker T. Washington, the president of Tuskegee Institute in Alabama, who advocated industrial training for blacks and accommodation to segregation.

Despite his long-standing criticism of accommodation to segregation, Fortune served as a ghost writer for Booker T. Washington, whom Republicans and white segregationists promoted as the most important black leader after Frederick Douglass. In

1900 Fortune and Washington organized the National Negro Business League, which remains active today.

Fortune's influence was such that American newspapers adopted "Afro-American," a term he invented to replace *Negro*, a Spanish word for "black" associated historically with slavery and a racial slur ("nigger"). Fortune's association with Booker T. Washington, however, tarnished his image among more militant blacks and the influence of the *Age* declined. Even though *The Age* had an average weekly circulation of six thousand in the 1880s (as compared to nine thousand for *The New York Times* in 1896) and was long subsidized by Booker T. Washington, the paper could not make sufficient profit for Fortune to stay out of debt. Fortune's failure was not unusual, however, for no black paper before 1895 had sufficient advertising or subscriptions to pay for more than a fraction of its costs.

In 1906 Fortune was declared legally bankrupt. He quarreled with Booker T. Washington, who would no longer see him and even declined Fortune's request for a loan to pay his rent. He sold the *Age*, sank into depression and alcoholism and became a homeless street drifter. In 1911 after obtaining professional and medical help, he recovered enough to rejoin the *Age*, this time as a salaried writer.

In the final years of his life, he wrote for the *Norfolk [Virginia] Journal and Guide* and edited black nationalist leader Marcus Garvey's newspaper, *Negro World*. While Fortune praised Garvey's leadership and positive attitude about blacks, he remained a supporter of racial integration.

At the end of his life Fortune no longer believed that racism could be absolutely eradicated. He concluded finally that the evil of racism, like other harmful aspects of human nature, could be suppressed by specific antiracist laws and by education, but would not disappear so long as there were recognizable races. He was among the first group of black publishers and editors to consider racism, like homicide, theft, and rape, a crime.

Shortly before Fortune's death in 1928 at the age of seventy-two, the National Negro Press Association praised him as the "dean of Negro journalism," whose writings would remain to guide blacks long after his death. His questioning of racial bloc voting, his criticism of racial loyalty to one party, and his rejection of black investment in racial division—to name but three prominent themes in his writings—anticipated issues that are just beginning to be considered in the 1990s.

IX

A GIANT OF ADVOCACY JOURNALISM—IDA B. WELLS

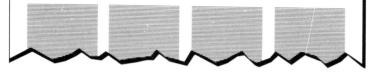

The Supreme Court had already repealed the Civil Rights Act of 1875, the day a conductor of a Tennessee rail car ordered a well-dressed young black woman to sit in the "Colored Car." When Ida B. Wells refused, he dragged her out of the "White Car." Ida sued the railroad company, but her first lawyer, a black man, made a deal behind her back with the company. An abolitionist white lawyer won a judgment of five hundred dollars for her, but the company appealed the award to the state supreme court, which dismissed the initial judgment. However, money generated by her write-up of the case in *The Living Way*, a religious newspaper, reimbursed her for her judicial setback. Unfortunately, during Reconstruction she and other blacks had few victories to celebrate.

Ida B. Wells had been born in a period of change. Her parents had been slaves in Holly Springs, Mississippi, where Ida B. Wells was born July 16, 1862.

She had no memory of slavery, except what she learned from her mother and father. Her mother, a half-Indian woman born in Virginia, related how the slaves' white mistress, "Miss Polly," had ordered slaves beaten and tortured for the slightest annoyance. Ida's father, Jim Wells, was the son of his master and a slave woman. No doubt her father's relationship to Miss Polly's husband accounted for the white woman's cruelty to Ida's parents. Ida's father was embittered by his former owners, despite having blood ties to them, and after the war he refused Miss Polly any contact with his family and himself. Miss Polly's repeated requests to see her husband's racially mixed grandchildren fell on deaf ears.

Ida, an avid reader, had read newspapers to her father before she had any formal schooling. Later she attended the freedmen's school, was a regular churchgoer, and assisted her mother with raising her seven brothers and sisters. During a yellow fever plague in Mississippi in 1876, Ida lost her parents and two of her brothers. When neighbors tried to put the other children up for adoption, Ida barred them from entering the house. She intended to preserve her family of brothers and sisters. Luckily, her father had been in the Fraternal Order of Masons, an organization pledged to assist the families of its members. Through the Masons, Ida found a job as a teacher at the country elementary school. At sixteen Ida was not only parent to her brothers and sisters but a teacher earning twenty-five dollars a month, who had to ride a mule six miles to work each day.

At the end of the school term, Ida and her siblings moved to Memphis, Tennessee, where relatives cared for her brothers and sisters and Ida found another teaching position. In Memphis, Ida attended Rust

College (later Shaw University) and Fisk University.

At this time she began writing articles for *The Living Way*, and writing a column under the pen name "Iola" for *The Gate City Press* of Kansas City, Missouri. She also contributed pieces to the *American Baptist*, the *Memphis Watchman*, the *Detroit Plaindealer*, and several other weeklies. In 1889 her life entered a new and exciting phase when she assumed control of the newspaper, the *Free Speech and Headlight* in Memphis. She ran a series of exposés of the school board, she defended the morality of black women against the smear of prostitution, and she attacked the "understanding clause" test designed to prevent blacks from exercising their Fifteenth Amendment right to vote. Black ministers who abused their position by seducing female members of their church also were targets of her muckraking paper.

The lynching of three blacks in Memphis in 1891 brought her career in the South to an end. Three blacks had been hanged by a white mob after an innocent quarrel over a game of marbles. The white papers of Memphis ran lurid headlines depicting the blacks as fiends, and as the violence spread, many black families fled Memphis for Oklahoma. Those who were left behind feared to speak out against the persecution. But despite threats from local white authorities, Wells continued to publish accounts of attacks on innocent persons and the reasons for the black flight from Memphis. It was a desperate and dangerous time for her, because now white southerners were overtly hostile to educated blacks.

On May 27, 1892, while Ida was travelling in the North, the *Free Speech* office was destroyed by a white mob. T. Thomas Fortune had invited her to New York City to discuss a business proposition.

"Well," he said. "We've been a long time getting you to New York, but now you are here I am afraid you will have to stay."

At first Wells thought Fortune was speaking oddly or teasing her.

"I can't see why that follows," she said.

"Well," he said, "from the rumpus you have kicked up I feel assured of it. Oh, I know it was you because it sounded just like you."

"Will you please tell me what you are talking about?" she asked.

"Haven't you seen the morning paper?" he asked.

"No," said Wells.[1]

Fortune handed her a copy of the New York *Sun*, where he had circled an Associated Press dispatch from Memphis. The article reported that the office of the *Free Speech* had been sacked and that the business manager, J. L. Fleming, had been run out of town. A note, read the article, was posted on the building warning that the publisher of the paper would face death if she returned.

Wells rushed immediately to a telegraph office with Fortune right behind her. She contacted her lawyer in Memphis, who confirmed the dismal news, but assured her that the paper's employees and their families were safe. He advised Wells not to return to Memphis and described in lurid detail how white lynch mobs combed the bus and train terminals, manhandling black women, while looking for her. A flood of telegrams followed from Wells's friends and neighbors begging her not to return to Memphis and to get a bodyguard, for her friends feared that the whites in Memphis would hire an assassin to kill her in the North. Of course, once she learned of the threat to her life, she could not go back to Memphis. Her life in the North began.

In her autobiography, Wells describes how she

accepted the end of her life in Memphis, at the age of thirty taking a

---

position on the New York Age [*to*] *continue my fight against lynching and lynchers. They had destroyed my paper, in which every dollar I had in the world was invested. They had made me an exile and threatened my life for hinting at the truth. I felt that I owed it to myself and my race to tell the whole truth.*[2]

In 1892, Fortune not only hired her as a staff writer and as a general reporter for the New York *Age* but, in return for *Free Speech* subscription lists, also gave her one-fourth interest in the *Age*.

Wells had come to Fortune highly recommended by two men who were never known to agree on anything: Booker T. Washington, and Boston *Guardian* editor William Monroe Trotter. As a reformer, a courageous defender of black civil rights, and a fine writer, Ida Wells was already something of a celebrity, known nationwide for her newspaper the Memphis *Free Speech and Headlight* and her editorials attacking lynching in criminal cases involving black defendants. Fortune himself reprinted her articles from *Free Speech* and used them freely in his *Age*.

Her first assignment at the *Age* was a seven-column front-page article on lynchings and rape. She described the sordid history of the white rape of black women which debased blacks and contributed to a public attitude that black women were immoral. Fortune had ten thousand extra copies printed of the edition containing Wells's analysis. One thousand copies of the paper were sold in Memphis alone.

Wells lectured widely on the subject of racism

and lynching. Antiracist groups in England and Scotland invited her abroad in 1893, and Wells began a series of highly influential lectures in Great Britain. She took Britain by storm, becoming a sensation in the press and gaining the admiration of both the common people and the aristocracy. Her trip was doubly successful in that she exposed the visiting American head of the National Women's Christian Temperance Union, Miss Frances Willard, as a racist, revealing how even leaders of progressive reform movements, including feminist Susan B. Anthony, were not immune to racism.

She was not afraid to explore difficult subjects, even delicate subjects like white-black unions. Many northern and southern whites feared so-called biological contamination by blacks through intermarriage or sexual union. A new word, *miscegenation*, had grown in usage since its creation by two racist Democratic journalists in 1864. Miscegenation referred to interracial marriage and mulattoes, to children of mixed racial ancestry. (The word *mulatto*— from the Spanish for mule—arose because some whites believed that mixed-race children, like the offspring of donkeys and horses, could not reproduce.) White demagogues sought to increase white hostility to blacks by pointing out the perils of mixed marriages, even though slavery, when white men prostituted black women, had been the real source of miscegenation and mulattoes.

Frederick Douglass confided in Ida B. Wells and was grateful for her kindness. Douglass had married Helen Pitts, a white woman, and was ostracized by many black women for not marrying a black woman.

"I want to tell you," he said to Wells, "you are the only colored woman save Mrs. Grimke who has come into my home as a guest and has treated Helen as a hostess has a right to be treated by her guest. Each of the others, to my sorrow, acted as if she expected my wife to be haughty or distant, and they all began by being so themselves."[3]

Wells was furious at the women for their bad manners and cruelty.

"Oh, Mr. Douglass," said Wells, "I am so sorry to hear that the women of my race committed such a breach of good manners. . . . I certainly deserve no credit for what I have been taught is ordinary good manners. The fact that Mrs. Douglass is white has nothing to do with it."

Douglass warmly thanked her. "I only wish," said Douglass, "everyone thought and acted as you do, my dear."[4]

What angered Wells more than anything else, even beyond the hypocrisy of blacks who practiced the kind of racial discrimination that they condemned in racist whites, was that as many whites as blacks made Helen Pitts suffer for her marriage.

Racist theories were in vogue. Educated blacks were unable to avoid exposure to all the writings in defense of racism. *The Atlanta Constitution*, for instance, then as now the major southern daily, editorialized regularly that "the supremacy of the white race must be maintained forever. . . . because the white race is the superior race."[5] Moreover, an intelligent and illiterate black person found little hope in either major political party. None but white radical politicians appealed to blacks, since the radicals at least preached racial justice, even if some of them privately held racist views.

X

RADICALS AND NATIONALISTS

"Every man should be glad that he is a Negro," wrote John Mitchell in *The Richmond Planet* in 1890. "The very oppression which is being forced upon him like a pall is working wonderful results, trying him in the furnace of fire and bringing him out a new race regenerated and redeemed. Who wouldn't be a Negro!"[1] Upholding freedom and black pride, Mitchell's militant tone reflected a nearly unanimous sentiment of black editorials: "You may say what you will, the Negro is here to stay. Nothing goes on without him. He was in the Revolutionary War, the War of 1812, the Mexican War, the War of Rebellion, and will be in everything that will take place in this country. Great is the Negro."[2]

When the image of blacks suffered in the white media, John Mitchell's newspaper, *The Richmond Planet*, published news of black achievements as a counterimage.

The Richmond Planet celebrated the achievements of the race in concrete terms:

Every time we see a Negro physician, it does us good. When we see a Negro pharmacist, it goes still better. When we see Negro lawyers, professors, bank presidents, inventors, machinists, skilled mechanics as well as linguists, we grin as much as our mouth will allow and shout—the Negro is coming.[3]

Mitchell's viewpoint was not uncommon, and the training of black skilled workers and professionals became a central theme of the black press and black leaders.

BOOKER TALIAFERRO WASHINGTON

On September 15, 1895, Booker T. Washington, the founder of an Alabama industrial training school for blacks and native Americans, Tuskegee Institute, spoke at the Cotton States Exposition in Atlanta and suddenly became the most powerful black spokesperson in the country. Declared Washington:

We began at the top instead of at the bottom. . . . A seat in Congress or the state legislature was more sought than real estate or industrial skill. . . . No race can prosper till it learns that there is as much dignity in tilling a field as in writing a poem. . . . In all things that are purely social we can be as separate as the fingers, yet one as the hand in all things essential to mutual progress.[4]

In his speech, Washington accepted second-class citizenship for blacks and harshly criticized efforts to force white toleration of black equality. The speech was hailed by President Theodore Roosevelt and the white press, not to mention Southern racists in the Congress. Because of his speech, Washington received honorary degrees from Harvard and Dartmouth colleges. Such public sanction of Washington deeply offended Boston's Harvard-educated editor William Monroe Trotter and W. E. B. DuBois, a well-known writer, who argued that blacks needed "a talented tenth" of highly educated blacks, politically uncompromising toward white racism. Trotter and DuBois held views that were utterly opposed to Washington's reluctance to criticize white racism.

In thirty years, Washington had risen from slavery to become the most powerful black leader in the country. He was invited to dinner at the White House by Theodore Roosevelt, who gave Washington veto power over black appointments in the government. Trotter became intensely critical of Washington's views and influence with white leaders. But there was little that either he or other militants could do. They had no newspaper or publication to present the black radicals' case.

In the North and West blacks had to face mainly white social attitudes, class values, and clannish ethnic politics. Unpleasant as northern whites might be, the absence of legal forms of discrimination in the North enabled many blacks like Monroe Trotter and

W. E. B. DuBois to receive the best education that the nation could offer. Trotter and DuBois, having grown up in integrated communities, were hardly disposed to accept lynchings and the denial of civil rights on grounds of race. While a lifelong accommodation to racism made most blacks unwilling to risk worsening their condition by challenging the system, blacks who had been integrated would not allow violence and intimidation to segregate or to humiliate them.

WILLIAM MONROE TROTTER

Monroe Trotter had been born April 4, 1872, in Boston. (His father, James Monroe Trotter, like the fathers of T. Thomas Fortune and Ida B. Wells, was the son of a slave woman and her white master). Monroe was educated at Harvard College and was the first black to be elected to Phi Beta Kappa in his junior year. He graduated magna cum laude in June 1895, three months before Booker T. Washington's famous Cotton States Exposition speech in Atlanta.

Trotter wrote in one letter that:

The conviction grew upon me that pursuit of business, money, civic or literary position was like building a house upon the sands, if race prejudice and persecution and public discrimination for mere color was to spread up from the South and result in a fixed caste of color. . . . As the American Jew and Irish have, and must save their own people in Europe, so must the northern Negro save himself by fighting the battles of the southern Negro.[5]

He joined a spontaneous development of black journalists and publishers such as the country had not witnessed since before the Civil War. The *Guardian*, which was to be Trotter's life's work, emerged as a powerful rallying voice for black aspirations. From 1900 to 1920, the paper gave Trotter both notoriety and prominence as a militantly uncompromising figure.

One of Trotter's first victories against racism was a small one, but it gave him national attention. Perhaps the greatest popularizer of white racism was author Thomas Dixon, a Baptist minister, whose sensational bestselling novels, *The Leopard's Spots* (1902) and *The Clansman* (1905), described blacks as a "menace . . . throwing the blight of its shadow over future generations, a veritable Black Death for the land and its people."[6] In *The Clansman*, Dixon exploited white sexual stereotypes of black lust. One of the most sensational scenes in the novel is of a black chasing and raping a terrified white virgin: "A single tiger spring," wrote Dixon, "and the black claws of the beast sank into the soft white throat." The black tormentor met justice of course from the end of a Ku Klux Klan rope. His victim and her mother committed suicide for suffering the ultimate form of debasement of a white woman.[7]

The Clansman was adapted into a feature film, *Birth of a Nation*, by film legend D. W. Griffith. The film depicted the Klan as protectors of white women. Civil rights organizations rallied at Boston theaters in 1905 to protest the outrageously racist film. The promoters of the film, however, had managed to have a private White House viewing for President Woodrow Wilson, who exuberantly recommended it: "It is like writing history with lightning," said Wilson, addressing himself to the technical form more than to the film's story. Critics responded that if the film was history, it was "history upside down, a complete inversion of the truth."[8]

Trotter led the Boston black protest against the film. Then managing editor of the *Guardian*, he organized intense pressure on Boston Mayor James Michael Curley to delay showing the film until hearings could be held to determine whether the film should be banned in Boston. When Griffith appeared at the hearing to defend the film, Trotter and other blacks nearly attacked him as well as his film.

Griffith offered ten thousand dollars to anyone who could show that the film was historically inaccurate. But he conceded that one scene in which a black soldier coerced a white woman into marriage was false. Although Trotter failed to prevent the film from being shown, he won national attention and praise from most black leaders, with the exception of his foe Booker T. Washington. Trotter had ridiculed Washington's views in person and in the paper.

Trotter was not awed by titles and directly confronted President Woodrow Wilson over segregation of federal facilities. Seeing racism as a worldwide problem, he promoted racial solidarity among nationalist movements in the Philippines, Haiti, and Cuba, which the United States invaded and exploited. He supported the Niagara movement, which led to the creation of the National Association for the Advancement of Colored People (NAACP). His flaws were that he could not tolerate subordinating himself to the leadership of others; nor could he tolerate dissent, nor delegate responsibility, nor manage subordinates. Working with others, it seemed, was difficult for Trotter for few people could match his exacting standards. In 1907 he established his own organization, the National Equal Rights League, like the *Guardian* predominantly a one-man operation.

SOUTHERN HORRORS

LYNCH LAW

IN ALL

ITS PHASES

MISS IDA B. WELLS,

Price, · · · Fifteen Cents

Ida B. Wells used black newspapers to expose
the terrorism of the Ku Klux Klan and its
lynching (hanging) of black men. This poster
from *The New York Age* advertises a speech
given by Ida B. Wells on the horrors of lynching.

W.E.B. DuBois was a leading black
intellectual who helped found
the NAACP and was the editor
of its monthly journal, *The Crisis*.

THE CRISIS

A RECORD OF THE DARKER RACES

Volume One   NOVEMBER, 1910   Number One

Edited by W. E. BURGHARDT DU BOIS, with the co-operation of Oswald Garrison Villard, J. Max Barber, Charles Edward Russell, Kelly Miller, W. S. Braithwaite and M. D. Maclean.

CONTENTS

PUBLISHED MONTHLY BY THE

National Association for the Advancement of Colored People

AT TWENTY VESEY STREET   NEW YORK CITY

ONE DOLLAR A YEAR   TEN CENTS A COPY

The front page of the November 1910 issue
of *The Crisis*, the journal of the NAACP

Black World War I soldiers.
The U.S. military segregated
black soldiers until 1953. The
black press publicized the
achievements of black soldiers.

Marcus Garvey, born on the island of Jamaica, was the leader of the Back to Africa movement in the United States following World War I.

These soldiers of an all-black defense battalion of the Marine Corps fought in the South Pacific during World War II. Desegregation of the army did not occur until after World War II. Coverage of black soldiers during the war was important in the growth of black newspapers.

Gordon Parks, one of the first black photojournalists to work in the white-owned media, was also a successful moviemaker and author.

The career of Carl Rowan, shown here with President Kennedy in 1963, has spanned many decades. In the 1990s, Rowan's column is syndicated in hundreds of American newspapers and Rowan appears regularly on network television.

John Johnson built his company, which publishes *Ebony* and *Essence* and many other black magazines, into a billion dollar black media empire. Johnson is shown here with his daughter, Linda Johnson Rice, the president of the company.

Among the many results of the
agitation for civil rights was the
integration of nonwhite journalists
into the mainstream white media.

THE PROBLEM OF COOPERATION

"Most colored papers," observed the publisher Reverend E. R. Carter of Atlanta's *The Black Side*, "start (after great advertising) with a boom, then peter out."[9] A black person who traveled around the country in the latter part of the nineteenth century would have probably agreed with the Reverend Carter. The pattern of many new black publications was not encouraging, since so many failed within a few months of their inception.

Even so, the black press had a number of successes, not least the product that Fortune and Wells were putting out. Other successes were *The Philadelphia Tribune*, established in 1884, which criticized "affluent middle-class Negroes"; the Baltimore *Ledger*, later Baltimore's *Afro-American*, published by a fence painter, John H. Murphy, Sr.; John Mitchell's *Richmond Planet*; and *The Christian Record*, a pre–Civil War religious journal of the African Methodist Episcopal Church. Still, all black papers had to overcome black apathy.

One black paper, *The Virginia Star*, criticized the lack of black subscriptions: "Colored men! You say you are as good as white men. If white men support scores of newspapers in this state, can you not support one? If you cannot, you do not prove that you are as good as white men."[10]

Black papers competed vigorously for white subsidies and black subscriptions. So many papers— concentrated mainly in five cities—meant financial ruin for most publishers and even a merger often could not save a paper whose subscribers were "social parasites," as one editor called those who took the paper without paying. "The difficulties," writes one critic, "Negro publications encountered emphasized the weaknesses within the black community."[11]

W. E. B. DUBOIS AND INTERNATIONAL RACIAL STRUGGLE

William Edward Burghardt DuBois (pronounced *Du-Boyce*) had been born in 1868 in Great Barrington, a town of five thousand in the Berkshires of western Massachusetts. Most of the fifty or so blacks who lived in the town had no memory of slavery and like the DuBois family were of mixed ancestry. Will, as the boy was called, was of French Huguenot, Dutch, African, and Indian descent, and as he was later often to say proudly, "not one drop of Anglo Saxon."[12] DuBois recalled almost no experiences of segregation or color discrimination as a child. His family had been free since the American Revolution and socialized with the white native Protestants rather than the immigrants, Roman Catholics of Irish and German ancestry.

His schoolmates were mostly white, as were his friends. The only black in his high school of twelve, he was fondly received by the other black families in the town. Not only did he deliver T. Thomas Fortune's *Globe* to them, but he served, at the age of fifteen, as the *Globe* (later the *Freeman*) correspondent. Few reporters were as young as DuBois, but few people in Great Barrington took their position as seriously as the boy, who also edited the *High School Howler* and contributed articles to the *Springfield Republican*. For one so young, DuBois displayed a seriousness and sense of responsibility out of proportion to his years. And he would be the only one of the town's few black students to go on to college.

Although DuBois graduated at the top of his high school class, he was encouraged to apply to a black college rather than nearby Amherst, Williams, and Harvard. DuBois illustrated here a curious aspect of black achievement, for by excelling over his white classmates he was to be further segregated. DuBois attended Fisk, a black college in Tennessee, which awarded him sophomore standing in recognition of his scholastic achievements. After graduation from Fisk, he did graduate work at Harvard University, and in 1892 he won a grant from the Slater Fund to study at the University of Berlin. He returned from Berlin two years later, and he received his doctoral degree from Harvard in 1895. He taught briefly at Wilberforce and Atlanta university, both black schools. Despite his excellent academic record, he was never to receive a formal appointment at a white university or college. Racial segregation of higher education meant that few blacks attended or taught at white colleges.

In 1895, DuBois became the chief spokesman for liberal education, particularly for blacks with exceptional intellectual ability, the so-called talented tenth. DuBois aggressively asserted the political and social equality of blacks. Washington secretly tried to discredit DuBois in newspaper editorials, principally written by T. Thomas Fortune. Washington and DuBois debated, in their writings and the writings of their supporters, the role of government in black progress. They were divided over whether blacks should first strengthen black economic and educational institutions or seek political freedom and equality. The debate meant little to the masses of blacks. Thousands of blacks agreed with neither DuBois nor Washington and for a majority the truth lay somewhere between the two extremes.

As early as 1900, DuBois had declared to a Pan-African Conference in London, "The problem of the twentieth century is the problem of the color line," in Africa, Asia, the Americas, and the islands of the Pacific.[13] Although he saw racism as a global problem, he never lost sight of the main priority of fighting it in his own country. The administrations of three presidents had done little to protect blacks from lynchings, riots, and segregation. Blacks had organized the National Afro-American Council (1903) and the National Association of Colored Women—to seek a means to act against racial oppression. The Equal Rights Convention, for instance, in 1900 had found that 260 blacks had been lynched in Georgia alone since 1885. W. E. B. DuBois had been teaching at Atlanta University during the worst period of white brutality to blacks. In 1905 he sent out a letter to black and white civil rights leaders to meet at Niagara Falls to discuss what action to take.

The meeting led to an organization that has since been called the Niagara movement. It remained a largely informal organization until a bloody race riot erupted in Springfield, Illinois, in 1910. The organization then incorporated itself as the National Association for the Advancement of Colored People (NAACP), bringing along nearly all the members of the Niagara movement. DuBois was the only black officer of the NAACP and the first editor of its journal, the *Crisis*. He proposed that "persistent manly agitation is the way to liberty."[14]

DuBois had written in *The Atlantic Monthly*, in a remarkably prophetic essay "The African Roots of War," May 1915, that the European countries and America would go to war over control of Africa's precious minerals and rubber. For the rest of his life, DuBois continued to present an international angle on racism in his journalism and scholarly work.

After World War I, DuBois concluded that blacks ought not to depend on either white radicals or unions, but rather ought to strengthen ties between the U.S. civil rights movement and anticolonialist movements abroad. He saw no better platform for

publicizing the fight against racism than the Paris
Peace Conference in 1919, which followed the allied
Victory over Germany. For black leaders the Peace
Conference was an opportunity to expose racism and
by appearing before the white powers to make their
appeal directly to the world. But the State Department disappointed most of the blacks and denied
visas to the black leaders who wanted to attend the
conference in Paris. One of the exceptions was the
NAACP's editor of the *Crisis*. DuBois sailed to
France on the official press boat *Orizaba* as one of a
handful of black correspondents to attend the conference at Paris. At this time he organized a Pan-
African Congress in Paris attended by black repre-
sentatives of fifteen countries in Africa, South America, the Caribbean, and Asia. One of its resolutions
declared:

*Wherever persons of African descent are civi-
lized and able to meet the tests of surrounding
culture, they shall be accorded the same rights
as their fellow citizens. They shall not be denied on account of race or color a voice in their
own Government, justice before the courts and
economic and social equality according to
ability and desert (failing which) . . . it should
be the duty of the League of Nations to bring
the matter to the attention of the civilized
world.*[15]

When DuBois returned to the United States in
March 1919, he pronounced the Congress a success:
"We got, in fact, the ear of the civilized world. . . .
The world-fight for black rights is on!"[16]

XI

THE CHICAGO DAILY DEFENDER AND THE PITTSBURGH COURIER

A nineteenth century Asian visitor to the United States, Mr. Wu Ting-Fang, reported that "lynching" was a curious American institution, "where police protect the mob rather than the prisoners."[1] By the turn of the century many black men were defending themselves against these attacks. Black people in New York City had defended themselves in race riots in the summer of 1900.

A market for black publishers depended on racial loyalty, and nothing created loyalty like outrage. Two of the most successful black publishers were extraordinary men—Robert Sengstacke Abbott, publisher of the *Chicago Daily Defender*; and Robert Lee Vann, publisher of the *Pittsburgh Courier*—who were prepared to profit from race conflict and the racial aspirations of blacks.

THE FIRST SUCCESSFUL BLACK NEWSPAPER:
the *Chicago Daily Defender*

The man who created the first major successful black newspaper was hardly someone who would stand out in a crowd. Robert Abbott was small, only five feet six inches, and plain looking and appeared to be unmistakably of West African tribal ancestry. His favorite dress was a top hat, cut-away coat, striped trousers, spats, white gloves, and a gold-headed cane. He chain smoked cigars, large Cuban "stogies." Mild and soft-spoken, he gallantly introduced himself, kissing the hands of ladies.[2]

By his guess Abbott had been born three years after the Emancipation Proclamation had freed the slaves, including his parents on St. Simons Island, just off the coast of Brunswick, Georgia. When freedom came, his father had already abandoned the family, and his mother, Flora Butler Abbott, was left to raise Robert alone.

Flora Abbott's second husband, John J. Sengstacke, had been the son of a wealthy German merchant and the slave woman the merchant had married. When his German father died after the Civil War, John Sengstacke was deprived of his inheritance by the former Confederate authorities in Savannah. John Sengstacke had been raised in Germany but returned to Savannah in a futile attempt to claim his inheritance. There he met and married the beautiful widow Flora Abbott.

Abbott's first exposure to newspaper work was in a part-time job at a print shop of the Savannah *Echo.* Abbott's stepfather became a German-English translator for Savannah's white-owned *Morning News.* Later his stepfather founded his own paper, the Woodville *Times*, where Abbott and his brother Alexander helped with the paper's typesetting, printing, collating, and delivery. When Abbott finished high school, he attended a succession of colleges, working at odd jobs. Hampton Institute where he studied printing, as well as academic subjects, awarded him a degree in 1896. He went to work for the Woodville *Times* and the *Echo*, since opportunities on white-owned newspapers were virtually closed to all black applicants.

The South was the poorest part of the country, and Robert could not find a printing job that paid a living wage. He moved north and enrolled in Chicago's Kent Law School where he was the only black in his class. After completing his studies, however, he found that racial discrimination prevented him from becoming licensed to practice law. An equally dark-skinned black journalist, Nick Chiles of the Topeka *Plaindealer*, told Abbott he would starve to death if he attempted to practice law. A fair-skinned prosperous lawyer in Chicago warned Abbott that he was "a little too dark to make an impression on the courts of Chicago."[3] So "Black Abbott," as he was later called by friends, learned that he faced a double form of discrimination. Frustrated at not practicing law, he drifted around the country, working odd jobs, even teaching, until one day a friend got him a regular printing job in Chicago.

With three black papers, the *Broad-Ax, Illinois Idea,* and *Conservator,* the forty thousand black residents of the windy city had more of a choice of papers than people in most towns of a similar size. The last thing black Chicagoans probably thought they needed was another paper. But Robert considered the three papers to be of such awful quality that another offering was needed. He quit his printing job, rented a room on State Street, borrowed a card table and a chair, and with his last quarter he bought a pencil and paper to compose the first published

Chicago Daily Defender, dated May 5, 1905. He obtained credit to pay for a print run of three hundred copies, which Abbott personally distributed door-to-door. "The Only Two-Cent Weekly in the City," the masthead boasted. The paper was four pages, the size of a large mail circular, and his staff was he and the teenage daughter of his landlady, Harriet Plummer Lee.

Despite his cultivated manner and reserve, Abbott was a tough and calculating businessman. Each week Abbott paid a printer $13.75 to produce three hundred copies. According to a description of the thirty-seven-year-old "newsboy":

Rain or snow, slush or mud, he carried a load [of newspapers] the length and breadth of the community, ringing doorbells and peddling the paper. Nights he visited every South Side barber shop, poolroom, nightclub, saloon, drugstore, and church, indeed anywhere Negroes assembled, selling papers and gathering news and advertising. He often was made the butt of coarse jokes, but he merely turned his head aside.[4]

"Black Abbott" became a familiar sight in the small black community on the South Side. He was so poor he padded his shoes with cardboard and had a steady diet of fried fish and tea. Later in the year Abbott obtained some paid advertisements, but the paper would have died in the first five years were it not for his landlady. Abbott could not afford his State Street room after a few months, so Mrs. Lee let him use her dining room, provided his meals, gave him money for small expenses, mended his clothes, and let him use her telephone. Years later Abbott would show his gratitude by hiring her daughter and surprising Mrs. Lee with a gift of an eight-bedroom house.

Just when news seemed flat and circulation was falling, a riot or lynching would provide sensational headlines to boost sales. When blacks fought heroically to defend themselves from attacks, sales shot up even more. Indeed, many of the counterattacks of blacks involved black soldiers. In 1906 black troops in Brownsville, Texas (the First Battalion, Twenty-Fifth Infantry, Companies B, C, and D), became incensed by the Jim Crow practices of the local whites and insulting signs on park benches, such as one that read "No Niggers and Dogs Allowed." When a black soldier was roughed up by local whites, his comrades shot up the town, wounding a policeman and killing a bartender. Because of white protest, President Theodore R. Roosevelt had all of the black enlisted men dishonorably discharged on November 5, 1906. Civilian blacks were outraged and found in the *Defender* a ready means to vent their anger over the injustice.

The *Defender*'s circulation was aided considerably by the immigration of nearly fifty thousand blacks from the South to Chicago in the decade before World War I. Many of the new arrivals were from Georgia, and they became loyal readers of the *Defender*. Abbott discovered that his fellow "Georgia Boys" liked sensational stories. In 1909, he began his first crusade against prostitution. The "against" position of his editorials contrasted with the titillating headlines of the reports, or "exposés." One headline read, "MOTHER TAKES INNOCENT DAUGHTER TO HOUSES OF ILL FAME," adding in small type underneath the headline, "to play the piano."[5]

In 1910, Abbott hired as editor J. Hockley

Smiley, a dandy with a handlebar moustache and a passion for good times, muckraking news, and sensationalism. Smiley became the first paid employee of the *Defender*.

The masthead of the *Chicago Tribune*, "World's Greatest Newspaper," became under Smiley's pen, the *Defender*'s masthead, "World's Greatest Weekly," to DuBois' call for an elite "talented tenth" to lead blacks, Abbott argued that "the black masses, not the black classes" were the true leaders.[6] Headlines included: "JIM CROW CARS RUNNING OUT OF CHICAGO DEPOT"; "WHITE GENTLEMAN RAPES COLORED GIRL,"[7] all in red ink. For the *Defender*, the news was always "race angled."

By the 1920s, the *Defender* had become a thriving business with a branch office in London. Abbott used black Pullman porters and railroad workers to distribute the *Defender*. White authorities often made life difficult for local distributors of black papers, but rail workers had regular travel schedules, and would deliver the paper because of "race loyalty." But Abbott also paid a good commission to his distributors.

As circulation increased, Abbott received death threats. Several cities in the South tried to ban distribution. Klan members burned homes of owners of copies. A riot occurred in Texas because a black teacher reported a lynching to the paper. Two correspondents were reported murdered and two others run out of town. Nevertheless with nearly a quarter million readers, Abbott could not only purchase his own printing plant for a half million dollars, but he also had no debts, and he was a millionaire. Furthermore, the *Defender* was the first unionized black paper and the first integrated one, with a white foreman and white advertising salesmen.

Abbott urged southern blacks to come north. His black migration campaign succeeded in drawing another 100,000 blacks to Chicago's South Side, the "Black Belt" (so-called because of the railroad tracks surrounding the district). With the increase in population, his paper thrived. The paper became a beacon of light to newly arrived black immigrants from the South. Nothing so pleased the publisher as to stand on a corner with a fresh cigar and discuss the race problem with anyone who came along.

One of the paper's curious features was the omission of "black" or "Negro" from its reports. Abbott, who had traveled to South America and been delighted by Latin American attitudes on race, insisted on referring to blacks as "race" people.[8]

Despite his sensational approach to news, Abbott believed in treating people with fairness. He was constantly issuing corrections to false reports and killing what he considered "trash." Then, too, he was eager to be accepted by Chicago's growing middle class, and there were limits to presenting what appealed to his "Georgia Boys." He once noted that if his employees and blacks in general acted decently, "the chances are we shall be treated decently."[9] Abbott tried to conduct his life and business by the Golden Rule. He never criticized publicly any employee, yet his written notes to them could be severe. His paper, according to social scientist Gunnar Myrdal, was "destined to revolutionize Negro journalism," and Abbott was "the greatest single power in the Negro race."[10]

Abbott chose the name *Defender* to emphasize the paper's role as an advocate of black progress and an adversary of racism. His career as a journalist permitted him at last to function as a lawyer for the race, a profession he had perhaps fortunately (at least as the readers of the *Defender* might argue) been denied so that he could serve a greater purpose.

The year that Robert Abbott hired his editor

Smiley, 1910, had been a fruitful one for black publishing. That year DuBois had begun the *Crisis*, P. B. Young, Sr., of Virginia had converted a fraternal newsletter into the Norfolk *Journal & Guide*, and Robert Lee Vann had started the *Pittsburgh Courier*, the only black paper to rival and surpass the success of Abbott's *Defender*.

ROBERT LEE VANN AND THE *PITTSBURGH COURIER*

Robert Lee Vann was of mixed background, of black, white, and Indian ancestors. He was born August 20, 1879, in Ahoskie, North Carolina, to Lucy Peoples, a former slave. Although Vann physically resembled an Indian or Asian, he refused to "pass" for any race but black. From an early age Vann was industrious and a good student. After high school, he attended Virginia Union University in Richmond and the Western University of Pennsylvania at Pittsburgh. After he graduated, he practiced law in the black community of Pittsburgh.

The *Courier*, which Vann described as a "two-page sheet initiated by a Negro in a pickle factory,"[11] had been the idea of Edwin Nathaniel Harleston, a guard at the H. J. Heinz food-packing plant. Harleston's partners in the paper, Edward Penman and Hepburn Carter, had a disagreement over the paper and brought in Vann to mediate. Within a short time, Vann, as the legal representative of the paper, was working more hours at the paper than at his law practice. Vann was active in Pittsburgh and Pennsylvania politics and became the city's first assistant solicitor (lawyer), a national representative of the NAACP, and eventually an assistant to the United States attorney general in the Justice Department.

But the *Courier* remained his full-time occupation until his death.

In the paper's pages appeared the work of some of the most influential black writers of the twentieth century, including black conservative George S. Schuyler; W. E. B. DuBois; NAACP secretaries Walter White, Roger Wilkins, and Carl Rowan; and one of the country's most famous photographers, Gordon Parks. The paper promoted black sports personalities like Joe Louis and Jackie Robinson. Vann broke through the southern ban on circulating northern black papers. His Washington political connections saw to it that blacks could obtain the paper without reprisal from local white authorities. With weekly editions in twenty cities from Florida to New York, the *Courier* campaigned against radio programs like "Amos 'n Andy" that demeaned the black image.

Vann's paper suffered a drop in circulation during the Great Depression, 1929–1939, but circulation continued to grow in the 1940s, as Vann extended his influence in Pittsburgh and Pennsylvania politics. The war years signaled an explosion of readership of his hard-hitting sensational paper, especially among black troops.

Robert Lee Vann died in October 1940, six months after Abbott's death. Vann left his paper to the management of his widow, Mrs. Jessie L. Vann, and his talented editor, P. L. Prattis, and business manager, Ira F. Lewis. At the time, the circulation of Vann's paper was 147,000, but nine years later the paper's readership had increased to 300,000, the largest of any black paper in the nation. Specially edited weekly issues of the paper were printed separately in Louisiana, Florida, Georgia, New York, Ohio, the District of Columbia, Detroit, Philadelphia, Cleveland, Chicago, and California. The paper's sales flourished among the black middle class. Although it sometimes carried sensational news items, accompanied by giant size headlines, its reporting was generally accurate.

The success of black papers like the *Courier* and the *Defender* owed much to the rise of black literacy and black militancy stemming from black experiences in World Wars I and II. By 1910 seven of ten blacks had become literate. At one time during the Second World War, the *Courier* deployed eight of its thirty-six black correspondents at the front. Because of the *Courier*'s efforts the government accredited the first black correspondent at the front, Edgar Rouzeau of the *Courier*, in 1942. There were no black photographers overseas, but the *Courier* had one of its reporters, Ollie Harrington, send back his action photographs. The *Courier* was the only black paper to send a white correspondent, Haskell Cohen, to write about the gallantry of black troops; however, the Baltimore *Afro-American* sent over the only black woman reporter, Elizabeth Murphy Moss. *The Pittsburgh Courier* led attacks on employment discrimination, military Jim Crow treatment of black troops, and military abuses during World War II.

While promoting patriotism, the *Courier* had denounced discrimination and segregation, thus making the black press a powerful voice for change.

XII

AFTER WORLD WAR I: MARCUS GARVEY

Abbott and Vann represented a new attitude among black journalists. Civil rights and equality were pursued by making appeals to white self-interest. Racism, the black publishers argued, hurt white pocketbooks too. Abbott actually organized black American boycotts of white stores that were not so easily dismissed as moral appeals. Public opinion, too, would be forced to take note of the criticisms of the United States coming from foreign lands. Indeed, black immigrant Marcus Garvey would galvanize black protest on a scale no other black American leader had ever achieved.

MARCUS GARVEY

Before Booker T. Washington's death in 1915, he had received a letter from a Jamaican asking to meet him at Tuskeegee. Washington received many such letters. He probably simply filed the letter and forgot about it. The letter's author, however, was to fulfill one of Washington's dreams of promoting black publishing. Like Washington, the author was a man of the people, raised in poverty and largely self-educated. His name was Marcus Garvey.

Garvey began as a printer's apprentice, at age fourteen, much like T. Thomas Fortune. A few years later he traveled through South America and England and was disheartened to find racism everywhere. After Garvey read Booker T. Washington's *Up From Slavery*, he wrote:

I read Up From Slavery *by Booker T. Washington, and then my doom—if I may so call it—of being a race leader dawned upon me. . . . I asked: "Where is the black man's Government? Where is his King and his kingdom? Where is his President, his country, and his ambassador, his army, his navy, his men of big affairs?" I could not find them, and then I declared "I will help to make them."*[1]

By the time Marcus Garvey sailed from Jamaica, the first black generation born in freedom was passing away. Men like DuBois, Trotter, and Fortune were nearing the age when people think of retirement. On March 23, 1916, Garvey disembarked in New York City from Jamaica on a gray and rainy day. He hoped to find support among black Americans for his organization, the Universal Negro Improvement Association (UNIA). Though the UNIA attracted very favorable publicity in Jamaica, the masses of blacks on the island were indifferent.

Garvey succeeded in enlisting support of promi-

nent blacks throughout the country and purchased a
string of small businesses; real estate in several
cities; a steamship line, the Black Star Line; the
newspaper *Negro World* with a circulation of two
hundred thousand; *Black Man* magazine; and the
monthlies *Negro Churchman* and *Negro Peace Echo*.
African-American membership in his UNIA rose to
100,000 and Garvey had bank accounts in the millions of dollars.

If blacks united in political elections and formed
black businesses, so the thinking of men like Garvey
went, they would be treated respectfully as white
ethnic groups such as Irish Americans and Jewish
Americans were. But other men like DuBois believed
just as firmly that blacks ought to assimilate fully
into white society, so that they would be indis-
tinguishable from whites and would not be vulner-
able to racial discrimination. Either way, as black
nationalists or as integrationists, the goal was to be
treated as whites were treated, to be respected for
group power, but not to be discriminated against
unfairly for being a member of the group.

The *Negro World* was begun in 1918, boldly pro-
claiming, "One Aim, One God, One Destiny: A Newspaper Devoted Solely to the Interests of the Negro
Race." Sections of the paper were in French and
Spanish for South American, African, and Caribbean
readers.

The front page proudly addressed itself to "Fel-
lowmen of the Negro Race" and was signed, "Your
obedient servant, Marcus Garvey, President General." The *Negro World* was filled with guest contrib-
utors, including T. Thomas Fortune. Editorials
extolled leaders of slave revolts Denmark Vesey and
Nat Turner, and the Haitian rebel leader Toussaint
L'Ouverture.

Garvey's editorials either promoted the UNIA or

proclaimed a grand future for blacks. "Africa must be redeemed," one editorial ran, "and all of us pledge our manhood, our wealth and our blood to this sacred cause. Yes, the Negroes of the world have found a George Washington, yea more; they have found a Toussant L'Overture [actual spelling], and he will be announced to the world when the time comes."[2]

The paper, ten to sixteen pages, contained news, opinions, and feature departments, of which poetry was the most popular. "Bruce's Grit" column by John E. Bruce and columns by T. Thomas Fortune were also popular. The paper refused advertising for skin-whitening and hair-straightening chemicals. Critics attacked the paper as the "Bulletin of the Imperial Blizzard," and "the *weakly* organ of Admiral Garvey's African Navy."[3]

Although Garvey's circulation figure of "400,000,000" was exaggerated, the paper had a profitable life, though the Justice Department placed it on a list of radical publications because of its militant editorials.

By the time W. E. B. DuBois, then *Crisis* editor, got around to examining Garvey's appeal, as well as his economic schemes, Garvey was considered by a large number of blacks to be the worthy successor to Booker T. Washington.

Garvey's editorials in the *Negro World* urged readers to abandon traditional middle-class leadership. He accused the NAACP and the Urban League of enriching the leaders at the expense of the working class. He harangued large street crowds in New York's Harlem. A genius in promoting himself, he was difficult to ignore. Once a thug assaulted his wife on the street, and Garvey himself chased the man away, an incident that became highly embellished and publicized in his hands.

His downfall began with two successful libel suits

against him. Garvey had written that a light-skinned editor of the radical *Crusader* magazine, Cyril V. Briggs, was a white man "passing for a Negro."[4] A lawsuit by Briggs forced Garvey to retract the statement and make a public apology.

Crisis editorials by DuBois challenged Garvey editorials for making false claims in *Negro World* about his steamship line. The Garvey editorials promoted the Black Star Line as worth $10 million, when, as DuBois demonstrated, the figure was simply on paper without actual money behind it. Eventually the shipping line failed.

The entry of the United States into World War I had raised blacks' expectations of social equality and respect from whites. Black troops were treated as heroes by the French and other Europeans, and when the soldiers returned to America they considered themselves equal to whites and were prepared to defend themselves against racism.

But black veterans of World War I were treated harshly for defending themselves. Racial tensions between Houston white police and black soldiers of the Third Battalion, for example, exploded on August 23, 1917. A shootout left twenty persons, four blacks and sixteen whites, dead. On December 11, 1917, nineteen black soldiers were executed and fifty were given life sentences.

The boll weevil pest had destroyed the cotton crops of the South in 1917, setting in motion a large migration of black southern workers to northern cities. Northern racism, however, had disillusioned many of the workers, who were stuck in the big cities and unable to return south. The major civil rights organization, the NAACP, mainly won legal victories for individual blacks, but their immediate impact on racism as a whole was slight.

Black radical publications appeared, especially

A. Philip Randolph's militant *Messenger*. Randolph and his Brotherhood of Sleeping Car Porters, one of the first black unions, were socialist in their goals, and Randolph placed his *Messenger* magazine at the service of the international socialist movement. As for lynching, Randolph insisted that blacks should "Always regard your own life as more important than the life of the person about to take yours. . . . "[5]

XIII

WORLD WAR II

The summer of 1919 became known as the "Red Summer," because so many race riots broke out in American cities. Poet Claude McKay expressed the resistance and militant sentiment of blacks in his poem "If We Must Die": "If we must die, O let us nobly die,/So that our precious blood may not be shed/ In vain; then even the monsters we defy/ Shall be constrained to honor us though dead."[1] Historian John Hope Franklin recalled noticing as a child that blacks in Tulsa had a new self-confidence after a 1920s riot there. In Chicago the *Defender* reported that a group of black separatists, the Abyssinians, had killed two whites in reaction to white bombings of black homes. Papers like the *Amsterdam News* and the *Baltimore Herald* promoted the "right of black self-defense."[2] The *Cleveland Gazette* and the *Washington Post*, for instance, deplored the views of Lexington, Kentucky's, black editor, the Reverend C. O. Benjamin, who in his paper called for blacks to unite and defend themselves after a lynching in Mississippi. Bleak as things were, blacks had made real and irreversible gains in organizing networks of information, the basis for political action.

In 1940 the National Negro Newspaper Publishers Association (NNNPA), a competitor with Claude Barnett's Associated Negro Press (established 1919), began to grow. Later the NNNPA became the National Newspaper Publishers' Association (with 148 member newspapers in 1989) and dropped "Negro" from its name. The Associated Negro Press, supplemented by twenty papers of the Negro Newspaper Publishers Association, imposed on black reporters and editors a dual obligation both to report the news and to attempt to influence governmental racial policies. Barnett's Associated Negro Press had been the first successful national and international news service for the black press and had become profitable because of new interest in Africa and the anticolonial struggle in the Third World.

WORLD WAR II

With World War II came an increased militancy in the black press and a wave of black riots, which would peak in the Detroit race riot of 1943. Membership in the NAACP skyrocketed from fifty thousand to a half million members in four years. Military service taught blacks the importance of organized efforts as nothing else had.

Black soldiers brought a new tone to race relations which white southerners were the first to notice. A mayor of one South Carolina town complained that the black press was responsible: "Since these damn Yankee soldiers have been coming down here, they've been putting hell in you niggers. I don't want one of those damn nigger papers sold around here."[3]

At least two army bases, Forts Rucker and Shelby, had banned the sale of black papers for a short time. But blacks were becoming increasingly important to the war effort, and the ban could not be sustained. In the spring of 1943, Tuskegee's Ninety-ninth Fighter Squadron had been put on active duty in North Africa, one year after the Marine Corps had admitted blacks for the first time. The four major black newspapers, the *Courier*, the *Defender*, the Baltimore *Afro-American*, and the *Norfolk Journal and Guide*, whose combined circulation was a half million readers, joined to create a "Victory at Home and Abroad Double V Campaign." They protested that the Office of War Information only released photographs of black troops digging ditches, lifting equipment, or peeling potatoes. With the NAACP's Walter White behind the papers, they succeeded in having the policy changed.

For many years the black press followed the lead of the Associated Negro Press (ANP), the *Defender*, and the *Courier* in coverage of news relating to Africa. During the Italian-Ethiopian War the *Courier* sent a black reporter, J. A. Rogers, to Ethiopia and Italy. The *Defender*'s man abroad was Dr. Willie N. Huggins. Few people would dispute historian John Henrik Clarke's judgment, that the black press has been more consistent in its coverage of Africa than any other American news medium. Reports of African personalities and independence movements stirred black American leaders to identify with the African anticolonialist struggle.

Black reporters generally had access to the news distributed at press conferences of the War Department branches, though they were barred from the president's press conferences and the Capitol Press

Galleries in the legislative branches. Access, however, was often not the most urgent concern of the black press. If they had an obsession, it was discrimination in the military as well as in the civilian sector. For instance, although a black physician, Dr. Charles Drew, had invented the technique for blood plasma preservation, the War and Navy departments forced the American Red Cross to segregate black and white blood donations, a practice that was not reversed during the war until it was exposed by black editorials. At the outset of World War II a general in the War Department's Public Relations Bureau labeled the Associated Negro Press (ANP) "lousy" for criticizing the department's mistreatment of black soldiers, particularly ANP's attacks on the department's exclusive use of segregated black units for logistical and service detail. Blacks had to fight for the right to fight, and the black press led the charge.

When War Secretary Henry Stimson argued in a letter to Congressman Hamilton Fish that blacks were not in combat because they "have been unable to master efficiently the techniques of modern weapons . . . (for reasons of) . . . lower educational classifications,"[4] the black press informally polled the embassies of other governments to see what the allies thought of Stimson's view of nonwhite abilities. Unanimously, the allies—Russians, British, and French, among others—stated that they had no problem using black and yellow men in combat roles. When the results of the black poll were published, the secretary reversed the policy, resulting in the activation of the 332nd Fighter Group (covered overseas by black correspondent Lemuel E. Graves, Jr., of Virginia's *Norfolk Journal and Guide*), the 477th Bombardment Group, and the 555th Paratroopers. Moreover, black press "harassment" of the department forced it to rescind segregated rehabilitation centers; to identify Dorie Miller, a black mess attendant, as a hero in the attack on Pearl Harbor; and to restore the Fair Employment Practice Committee to monitor discrimination in the United States Employment Service. Black correspondents such as Ernest E. Johnson of ANP focused the attention of the larger white media on the racism of particular officials, personally embarrassing and sometimes politically damaging them.

OTHER PAPERS

No account of the black press would be comprehensive without a mention of some of the papers which published continuously after World War I and had circulations in the 100,000 range. *The Call* of Kansas City, Missouri, begun in 1918 by Chester Arthur Franklin and his mother, had developed into a major voice of blacks in the Midwest. In keeping with its feminine inspiration, the paper had hired a woman managing editor in the 1930s, Lucille Bluford. *The Call* became the first American newspaper to join the Audit Bureau of Circulations, an organization which guarantees the quality and quantity of a newspaper's patronage. The paper's policy of emphasizing achievements of blacks won it financial success, readership, and influence. One of *The Call's* reporters, Roy Wilkins, would become the national secretary of the NAACP and one of the most influential men during the 1960s and 1970s.

The *Amsterdam News* of New York City, begun in 1909 by James H. Anderson, grew with the black New York population from an obscure sheet into a prestigious paper. The paper had been largely a business proposition since its inception, unique in black journalism, and became one of the most widely circulated black papers after the *Courier* and the Baltimore *Afro-American*.

As author J. Kirk Sale once wrote, The *Amsterdam News'* depiction of the seamy side of black life, its blatant appeal to black middle-class values, and its partisan editorials during times of racial tension provided "a window onto the black world" for non-blacks.[5] Unlike the *Defender* and the *Courier*, the paper had no air of a crusade. It was also the first black newspaper not to depend on local merchants for advertising revenues, and the first to obtain national advertising from white companies.

A major difference in newspapers before and after World War II was in the new extensive social coverage and the features on black life. In the 1950s, blacks who achieved prominence or notoriety were gossiped about regularly in the mass circulation papers, The *Defender, Afro-American, Courier,* and *Amsterdam News.*

A CRISIS PRESS

After the war, challenges to legal segregation by the NAACP and the National Urban League became front-page items. In the South, two violent race riots occurred in the late 1940s. During this period the Congress on Racial Equality and A. Philip Randolph abandoned the legal struggle for more direct action. Protesters led Freedom Rides in violation of segregated seating in public accommodations (buses, trains, drinking fountains, and restrooms). Together, protest and legislative action brought about the end of segregation in the military, the establishment of the Fair Employment Practices Commission, and a ban on legal housing discrimination. While black papers covered the crisis, they attempted to promote a positive view of black life.

Historian Roland E. Wolseley listed seven reasons for the upsurge of black papers:

1. Better education of blacks.
2. New earning power.
3. Social service and group support.
4. Increased propaganda needs or religious organizations.
5. Black political agitation.
6. Political influence of black editors.
7. Segregation of the black community so that blacks needed to protest as well as report on black life.[6]

Of those seven conditions, it was the last which accounted for the success of the first major black newspapers. Until blacks felt they had a common and overriding interest in racial unity, they could not appeal to blacks across differences of region, income, politics, education, and complexion.

XIV
A BLACK JOURNALISM EMPIRE

Black veterans, like many white veterans, had benefitted from free college and professional training provided by the GI Bill. Accordingly, the post–World War II black population was both more affluent and more literate than were blacks before the war. Whereas in 1940, the four major black newspapers— the *Amsterdam News, Pittsburgh Courier, Chicago Defender*, and *Norfolk Journal and Guide*—had combined circulations of 274,954, in 1947 the figure had more than doubled to 627,405. In 1948 blacks had 56 college campus publications, 100 religious and special interest periodicals, and 169 black newspapers— 4 of them with regional editions and total combined circulation of 4 million.

However, the major development in the black press during this time was not a newspaper, but the creation of a magazine empire, the Johnson Publishing Company owned by John H. Johnson, publisher of *Ebony, Jet*, and *EM*, a fashion magazine for men.

JOHN HAROLD JOHNSON AND *EBONY* MAGAZINE

John Harold Johnson was born on January 19, 1918, in Arkansas City, Arkansas, a small rural mill town. His father was killed in a mill accident when Johnson was six, and his mother, Gertrude Jenkins Johnson, married another mill worker. Johnson attended segregated elementary schools taught by ill-prepared black teachers, who taught three and four classes simultaneously in the same classroom. But Johnson was an ambitious, intelligent youth who valued what little education he received. Because Arkansas City lacked a high school for blacks, many of the other children in his class immediately went to work after receiving elementary school diplomas in the eighth grade. Even though Johnson had received his eighth-grade diploma, he wanted to learn more about the world. Rather than drop out of school to work in the mill, he repeated the eighth grade.

In 1933, Mrs. Johnson and her son visited the World's Fair in Chicago. They found living conditions for blacks in Chicago vastly improved over those in Arkansas, and she and her husband decided not to return to Arkansas. For eighteen months the family lived on welfare in the poorest South Side section of Chicago's Black Belt. Johnson, in one interview, said, "The other kids used to laugh at me and make fun of my homemade clothes. . . . I decided I would show 'em, and I did." His father obtained a job at the Works Progress Administration (WPA) and Johnson worked part-time under the New Deal's National Youth Administration program. He attended Du Sable High School, named for a black trapper who founded Chicago. In 1936, Johnson gave a talk, "America's Challenge to Youth," at the school. The president of one of the largest insurance companies, Harry H. Pace of Supreme Liberty Life Insurance Company, was in the school and heard Johnson speak. Pace was impressed with Johnson's command of the language and intelligence. The businessman encouraged Johnson to attend college and gave him a part-time job. Johnson did not disappoint Pace.

For the next two years, not only did Johnson attend the University of Chicago on a scholarship, but he began editing Supreme Liberty Life's company magazine, an in-house publication. It was then, in assisting Pace in publishing some news about blacks, that Johnson first had the idea of publishing his own magazine for blacks.

In 1942, he used his mother's furniture as collateral to borrow five hundred dollars from a loan company to send out a subscription letter offering twenty thousand readers a subscription to *Negro Digest* (later *Black World* magazine). When three thousand people sent in their checks, Johnson published the first issue of five thousand copies in November 1942. The magazine was a black version of *Reader's Digest*, filled with personal feature stories on topics ranging from the problems of the lovelorn to racial discrimination, most of it reprinted from other magazines and newspapers. The progress of the magazine was touch-and-go at first, with revenues hardly enough to pay the cost of printing. When sales were poor, Johnson had friends go to news dealers and ask them to buy the magazine, and the gimmick had dealers scrambling to buy Johnson's magazine. But when regular columns like "My Most Humiliating Jim Crow Experience" and "If I Were a Negro" did not increase subscriptions, Johnson began to look for an author with wide public appeal. He found the author in the wife of President Franklin D. Roosevelt, a social leader widely respected in the black as well as the white community. Eleanor Roosevelt contributed a piece for the "If I Were a Negro" column and subscriptions soared in the following months to 150,000.

Johnson's next publication, inspired by *Life* magazine, was a glossy monthly magazine emphasizing color photographs of black celebrities and entertainers. Because the magazine was about blacks, he called it *Ebony*, the name of an African tree prized by African wood sculptors for the dark brown finish and durability of its wood. The purpose of the magazine, said Johnson, was to

show not only the Negroes but also white people that Negroes got married, had beauty contests, gave parties, ran successful businesses, and did all the other normal things of life. . . . About 10 percent of the Negro people are those who are able to enjoy many of these advantages we're speaking about. . . . We are like the movies—just as they tend to embellish and adorn the normal. I think we do the same. This is not to misstate the truth but simply to express the search for something that will capture the imagination.[1]

Ebony promoted the black middle-class dreams of the good life. To that end, the magazine devoted most of its coverage to the lives and accomplishments of the glamorous and accomplished people in black society, or what DuBois described as "the talented tenth." Once when an employee complained that the magazine contained too much copy on entertainment, Johnson recalled that his mother always gave him orange juice when he had to take castor oil. The function of entertainment, in Johnson's view, was to get people to read the serious material in his magazine.

The first issue of *Ebony* magazine, November 1945, sold out the entire printing of twenty-five thousand copies. Still, without major advertising revenues, the magazine was hostage to the whims of readership fads. The history of black publishing offered little comfort to Johnson. Most publications dependent on black newsstand sales and subscriptions did not survive. Few black magazines had ever made the publishers wealthy, but quite a few had bankrupted the owners. In 1946, however, Johnson succeeded in persuading Zenith Corporation to buy advertising space, which led to automobile and liquor advertisements from other large white-owned corporations. *Ebony* became the first black publication to advertise the services and products of international white-owned corporations, in addition to advertising personal care products and general consumer merchandise.

Over the years *Ebony* was to shift its editorial slant to underscore black achievement. "Achievement in the old era," wrote Johnson on *Ebony*'s twentieth anniversary, "was measured to a great extent by material things. Today achievement is measured in terms of whatever a man sets out to do."[2] All aspects of black life and personalities, in literature, religion, politics, show business, art, sports, crime, military, business, civil rights, and education, appeared in four-color photo stories in *Ebony*. In 1967, the magazine became the first black monthly to pass the 1 million mark in circulation.

His attitude, he told a *Fortune* magazine writer, was "I don't want to destroy the system—I want to get into it."[3] And after the War he became more than a part of the business community. Johnson's strongest competition for black readers, ironically, was from a white publisher, George Levitan of Texas, the publisher of sensational tabloid thriller magazines for blacks (*Hep, Jive, Bronze Thrills*, and *Sepia* published by his Good Company).

Johnson's awards included ambassador-at-large during the presidency of Lyndon Johnson, the NAACP Freedom Award, the Horatio Alger Award, and the National Medal of Freedom. He and his wife, Eunice, married since 1941, have two adopted children. Johnson's daughter, Linda, has assumed the role of publisher of The Johnson Publishing Company, a book and magazine publishing conglomerate ranked among the country's top four hundred corporations, with assets in the hundreds of millions.

Johnson will be remembered for providing opportunity for many black photographers and journalists, as well as for reversing the negative image of black people.

XV

BLACK LIBERATION

World War II had revitalized a major theme of the black press, the civil rights struggle. The black press's in-depth reports of the weekly assaults on blacks, especially the NAACP's legal challenges to publicly humiliating forms of segregation, contributed to the dramatic rise in black readership. In the next decade, as the struggle spread to all areas of society, the main black interest in black journalism became the civil rights movement.

In a revolutionary ruling that reversed the *Plessy v. Ferguson* decision (*Brown v. the Board of Education of Topeka, Kansas*), the 1954 Supreme Court outlawed school desegregation. The Reverend Martin Luther King, Jr., and Rosa Parks began the Montgomery bus boycott to protest the separate accommodations for the races, and their struggle inspired college students of all races to demonstrate and protest with civil rights marches. But whites in segregated communities continued to resist integration. In 1957, President Dwight D. Eisenhower had to federally direct the State National Guard to integrate public schools in Little Rock, Arkansas. Government action, however, was too slow to satisfy a post-World War II generation of black college students and older activists.

Protest organizations sprung up in black communities across the nation. Groups such as the Congress on Racial Equality (CORE), the Southern Christian Leadership Conference (SCLC), and the Student Nonviolent Coordinating Committee (SNCC) led marches in massive campaigns of civil disobedience. President John F. Kennedy enforced the desegregation of the South, and after Kennedy's assassination, his successor, Lyndon Johnson, signed the first Civil Rights Bill ensuring blacks full legal equality.

All legal discrimination based on race was banned by the Civil Rights Act of 1964. The bill provided affirmative action provisions in employment, protecting women as well as blacks. As a result of his leadership role in the 1963 March on Washington (which led to the 1964 Civil Rights Bill), the Reverend Martin Luther King, Jr., received the Nobel Prize for Peace in 1964.

White violence took the lives of several civil rights workers in the South, including Medgar Evers, a Mississippi NAACP leader. Evers was allegedly assassinated outside his home by a white Ku Klux Klansman, a man acquitted by an all-white jury in the late 1960s. (On the basis of new evidence, the case was reopened by the Mississippi attorney general in 1990.) The press covered scenes of white mobs as they assaulted Charlayne Hunter, who was enrolling at the Journalism School of the University of Georgia, one of the first two black students in the 175-year-old school's history. (Today Charlayne Hunter-Gault is one of the senior correspondents on the "McNeil-Lehrer News Hour," an award-winning program on public television stations.) Events involving dramatic confrontations over integration were covered sensationally in the black and white presses. The public exposure demoralized congressional opponents of civil rights for blacks.

At the same time Elijah Muhammad published in the *Amsterdam News* a doctrine of black supremacy. Muhammad's message was a racial interpretation of Islam reported by a columnist named Minister Malcolm X. The column appealed to many blacks frustrated with the slow pace of racial integration. Out of Malcolm X's column the newspaper *Muhammad Speaks*, one of the most widely circulated 1960s black newspapers, was created.

Not since Marcus Garvey's publications had a black newspaper expressed antiwhite sentiment as had Elijah Muhammad's (1897–1975) *Muhammad Speaks*. Editorials in the paper and on black radio stations espoused militant opposition to racial integration. Pointing to his wholly black supported financial empire in Chicago and Detroit, Muhammad divided the civil rights coalition. He all but ended the popular notion that black organizations automatically supported integration.

Not long into the decade, Stokeley Carmichael of SNCC issued his cry, "Black Power." Black papers became divided over the issue of nonviolence. Editorials in previously integrationist papers like *The Courier* questioned the goal of integration. Moreover, many liberal whites abandoned President Lyndon Johnson's "War on Poverty," calling it ineffective and wasteful. White backlash, as the disillusionment and reaction of whites was called, led to widespread black despair of achieving equality with whites.

Yet developments in mainstream media showed that the future for integration was not altogether bleak. After years of extensively, and perhaps excessively, covering black responses to white resistance to integration, the 1960s white media had increasingly begun to report news about black life. The nation became aware of black journalists such as Mal Goode. In 1962, Goode achieved a double first, as the first black reporter hired at ABC network as well as the first black hired at any major television network. CBS network, following ABC's lead, had hired George Foster as correspondent and Lee Thornton as White House correspondent. Yet the media had no in-depth coverage of the range of black opinion. Many white Americans had learned from the media more about Europe than they had learned about the everyday lives of black coworkers and neighbors. As a rule, when most white media had not ignored black news, it had interpreted it from a blatantly racist angle. In a 1965 lawsuit brought by the United Church of Christ on behalf of Jackson, Mississippi's black community, Jackson's white-owned WLTB-TV station lost its broadcasting license because of its racist coverage of the March on Washington.

EMPLOYMENT OF BLACK JOURNALISTS

Throughout the 1960s, not only had the black press remained the traditional employer of nearly every black journalist, but the rare black journalist occasionally hired by the white media had been practically invisible to public view until after the sensational racial riots in Watts, Los Angeles in 1965 and 1966; Detroit; and Harlem in 1967, and the riots that occurred after the assassination of the Reverend Martin Luther King, Jr., on April 4, 1968, in Memphis. Suddenly the white media wanted black reporters to cover developments in the black community, and white newspapers needed black editors to interpret black news. White publishers sought out black business people to establish good relations with community leaders.

The National Advisory Commission on Civil Disorders (sometimes named the Kerner Commission for its chairman, Illinois Governor Otto Kerner) reported in 1968:

They [general media] have not communicated to the majority of their audience—which is white—a sense of the degradation, misery, and hopelessness of living in the ghetto. They have not communicated to whites a feeling for the difficulties and frustrations of being a Negro in the United States. They have not shown understanding or appreciation of—and thus have not communicated—a sense of Negro culture, thought, or history.

Equally important, most newspaper articles and most television programming ignored the fact that an appreciable part of their audience was black. The world that television and newspapers offered to their black audience was almost totally white, in both appearance and attitude. As we have said, our evidence shows that our so-called "white press" is at best mistrusted and at worst held in contempt by many Black Americans. Far too often, the press acts and talks about Negroes as if Negroes do not read the newspapers or watch television, give birth, marry, die and go to PTA meetings. Some newspapers and stations are beginning to make efforts to fill this void, but they still have a long way to go.[1]

The Kerner Commission had devoted an entire
chapter to the news media and black unrest, showing
how public information influenced racial attitudes.
Among other things, the commission's report had
criticized white media for hiring only one syndicated
black columnist, Carl Rowan, and for hiring fewer
than one hundred black journalists. In the words of
the commission:

*Journalism is not very popular as a career for
aspiring young [blacks]. The starting pay is
comparatively low and it is a business which
has, until recently, discouraged and rejected
them. The recruitment of [black] reporters
must extend beyond established journalists, or
those who have already formed ambitions
along these lines. It must become a commit-
ment to seek out young [black] men and
women, inspire them to become—and train
them as—journalists. We believe that the news
media themselves, their audiences and the
country will profit from these undertakings.
For if the media are to comprehend and then to
project the [black] community, they must have
the help of [blacks]. If the media are to report
with understanding, wisdom, sympathy on
the problems of the black man—for the two are
increasingly intertwined—they must employ,
promote and listen to [black] journalists.*[2]

One result of the riots and the commission's report, at the close of the 1960s, would be the creation
of the Program in Journalism for Members of Minority Groups, for training black journalists at Columbia University.

LOUIS LOMAX

One of the pioneering journalists of this period was Louis Lomax (1922–1970), a reporter on *The Afro-American* and syndicated columnist for the North American Newspaper Alliance. His coverage of the Montgomery, Alabama, bus boycotts, led by the Reverend Martin Luther King, Jr., had broken new ground in on-the-scene reporting of civil rights protests. Although he leaned toward radical politics (he was the first American to visit North Vietnam in 1966), Lomax had been conservative in journalistic practices, an honest man unafraid to change his mind as warranted by the facts. During the early 1960s, Lomax had claimed that the NAACP was obsolete and had been superseded by more radical groups like the Congress on Racial Equality (CORE), King's Southern Christian Leadership Conference (SCLC), and the Student Nonviolent Coordinating Committee (SNCC). During the 1960s civil rights struggle the role of television and television news personalities had greatly expanded in the black press, and Lomax joined traditional groups to aid the struggle by organizing televised fund-raising appeals. Today all manner of groups and causes use telethons, round-the-clock appeals for telephone pledges to television programs, to raise financing for their purposes. One of the first telethons ever to appear nationally, however, was produced by Louis Lomax for support of the Freedom Rides.

Lomax produced the first award-winning television shows by a black producer, "Walk in My Shoes" and "The Hate That Hate Produced," for the American Broadcasting Company (ABC). His book *The Reluctant African* (1960) had predicted separatist developments of the civil rights movement. Later events in the decade convinced him of the error of his earlier prediction. He had debated Malcolm X, who then urged racial separation. After learning more of traditional Islam's nonracial values and falling out with Muhammad, Malcolm X would change his name to Malik el-Shabazz and, just before he was assassinated, embrace Lomax's argument for integration. Lomax had opposed even self-imposed black segregation because of the profoundly new racial equality blacks had won in the courts.

CARL ROWAN

The dean of black journalists, of course, remains Carl Rowan, newspaper and television columnist. Rowan had become one of the first blacks to integrate the Navy officer corps in World War II; one of the first blacks to work for a major white newspaper, the *Minneapolis Tribune* (1948); the first black to serve as ambassador to Finland and as head of the United States Information Agency. His 1991 book, *Breaking Barriers: A Memoir*, hit the bestseller lists, and he has received innumerable awards. Along with Lomax, Rowan reported the civil rights developments of the 1950s and 1960s. Rowan also covered international developments in Asia, having been one of the first American journalists to visit Communist China—Boston journalist William Worthy was the first—and served as an expert on Asian affairs for the United States Diplomatic Corps.

XVI

TOWARD THE TWENTY-FIRST CENTURY

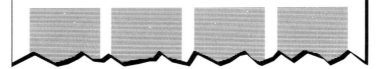

THE NEXT GENERATION

Although blacks have been making significant inroads into traditionally all-white ownership of media, less than 2 percent of commercial radio stations are black owned. Since the first black-controlled educational television station came into being (Howard University's WHHM, Channel 32, Washington, D.C.), the trend has continued toward black production of programs, rather than ownership or control. In the 1990s, Washington, D.C., based Robert Johnson's Black Entertainment Television Holdings, Inc. (BET), a cable network, became the first black-owned company to be publicly traded on the New York Stock Exchange.

In the 1980s, black publishers and executives had begun operating daily newspapers for predominantly white readers. Robert Maynard of the Oakland, California, *Tribune*, serving the readers of the ethnically diverse Oakland–San Francisco urban area, was the first black to buy a major metropolitan newspaper in the United States. A high school dropout, Maynard founded and administered the University of California's Institute of Journalism at Berkeley. When his paper was sold in the summer of 1992, the new owners, the Alameda Newspaper group, appointed Pearl Stewart, a black veteran reporter at the paper, as editor. Other achievers include the 1989 Pulitzer Prize winner and nationally syndicated columnist Clarence Page of the *Chicago Tribune*; *USA Today* editor Barbara Reynolds; Pam Johnson, publisher of the *Ithaca Journal*; and Ron Townsend, president of the Gannett Television Corporation. In 1993, the American Society of Newspaper Editors installed its first black president, William A. Hilliard, editor of the *Oregonian*. At Johnson Publishing, the daily operations of *Ebony, Jet, EM*, the monthly black men's magazine, three radio stations, and two lines of personal care products are in the hands of Johnson's daughter, Linda Johnson Rice. In the early 1990s, *Ebony* had a monthly circulation of nearly 2 million, while the company as a whole brought in nearly $250 million in revenue.

There has been a continuing demand for black publications, even with integration in the media. From Los Angeles to Boston, one finds an increase in black specialty magazines. As of August 5, 1990, there were twenty-five black-oriented magazines. "The increase in black-oriented magazines," says Samuel J. Chisholm, president of the Mingo Group, a New York advertising agency specializing in black consumers, "is a result of the varied interests in the black community. . . . "[1]

Typical of the magazines, Washington, D. C.'s, *American Visions* focuses on art, history, and culture; *Emerge* of New York concentrates on life-styles of the upper-middle class, while *Reach New England* aims at minority businesses in New England. The mainstay of women's fashion, of course, has been the New York based *Essence*, founded in 1970. None of the current magazines appear to be as ambitious as the Sunday supplement carried in white papers, *Tuesday*, founded in 1968, which was a black version of *Parade* and had a circulation of 1.4 million before folding in the 1970s. Though Earl Graves's *Black Enterprise Magazine*, which focuses on black achievement in all areas of business, has become a major commercial success, the trend toward more integration of blacks in the profession has continued.

At the Fifteenth Annual Convention of the National Association of Black Journalists, the main concern was "reaching out to break . . . the profession's final barrier . . . the top levels of management and media ownership." The association, which has 2000 members, complained that most newsrooms are "lily-white" and that segregation is especially evident in the news departments.[2]

As of the early 1980s, there had been only four nationally syndicated black cartoonists—not much of an increase since Alden S. McWilliams (1916–1993) created the "I Spy" comics and Elmer Simms Campbell (1906–1974) established a black presence in the highly competitive world of slick white-oriented magazines, *The New Yorker, Esquire, Cosmopolitan,* and *Redbook.*

Black photographers have begun to achieve recognition since the time of the early photojournalists. Keith Williams of the *Louisville-Courier Journal*, a Pulitzer Prize–winning photographer, participated with forty-nine other black journalists to produce the photo book *Songs of My People.* Williams followed the trailbreaking *Life* magazine photographer, Gordon Parks, born in 1912, whose autobiography, *The*

Learning Tree, and feature film of the book won many awards. Parks also produced the *Shaft* films. In 1960 he was named Magazine Photographer of the Year and awarded the Newhouse Award from Syracuse University in New York. Moneta J. Sleet, Jr., staff photographer for *Ebony*, won a Pulitzer Prize in 1969 for his photograph of Coretta Scott King at her husband's funeral. In 1975, the Pulitzer Prize winner for photography was Matthew Lewis, freelancer at the *Washington Post*.

THE ROLE OF BLACK ENTERTAINMENT

Besides advocating civil rights and reporting on the news, black broadcasting has joined black music and film companies to articulate a black style of life. Black television-news shows and black-owned radio stations have appeared in nearly every state of the union. Since Berry Gordy, the president of Motown Records, entered the Fortune Five Hundred List of American Millionaires, Motown has produced television features, including "Lonesome Dove," a highly acclaimed western viewed by a mainly white audience. Filmmakers Spike Lee (*She's Gotta Have It, Do the Right Thing, Mo' Better Blues*, and *Malcolm X*), Robert Townsend, Reginald Hudlin (*House Party*), and Keenan Ivory Wayans (*I'm Gonna Git You Sucka'* and the television comedy "In Living Color") have become household names.

FREE-LANCE JOURNALISTS

At the end of World War II Stanley Roberts of the *Pittsburgh Courier* had discovered that General Douglas MacArthur was in New York City but refused to grant news interviews. Roberts sent word to the general that some black newspapers—not the *Courier*, of course—were blaming MacArthur for the racial segregation in the United States military units occupying Japan. MacArthur immediately met with Roberts to deny the accusation: "They didn't send me enough of them," said MacArthur. Roberts had achieved a "scoop," leading to a two-part interview in the *Courier* and pieces in *Time* magazine and *The New York Times*. His achievement indicated that when black journalists succeed in getting a story of general interest, they will easily find a general audience, even when the subject affects black Americans most directly.

Not many journalists, black or white, have been successful freelancers, but the author Alex Haley (1921–1991), another Pulitzer Prize winner, was unique. His account of his family origins, *Roots: The Saga of An American Family* (1976), broke all television viewer ratings records in the United States when it appeared on network television. His collaborative *Malcolm X* autobiography became a 1992 hit movie, produced by Spike Lee. Probably no other journalist both won so many awards and reaped so much financial reward as Haley, for telling the story of how his African forebears came to America, survived slavery and racism, and reestablished bonds between Africans and African Americans.

Black journalists today have realized the fondest hopes of the early black pioneers, Russwurm and Cornish of *Freedom's Journal*. But without the sacrifices and selfless devotion of those inspired and dedicated publishers, who worked on sheer hope alone, the future for the black press would probably not seem so assured as it does today. When one views black documentaries and feature films such as the award-winning television documentary *Eyes on the Prize*, written by *Washington Post* columnist Juan

Williams and produced by Henry Hampton (a 1991 winner of a Silver Baton Award for television documentaries), one cannot help being moved by the enormous progress and triumph of the human will those programs represent.

Black journalists still face obstacles in training and employment, as well as in sustaining black owned media. But whether the main interest of a black journalist lies in print, broadcast, or freelancing, or whether the journalist wishes to work in an integrated or a black company, the opportunities and rewards are greater than ever. Today, fortunately, the question of whether to work in integrated or segregated media means a choice between a local or specialized market of consumers rather than a segregated workplace.

ENDNOTES

Preface

1. Frederick Detweiler, *The Negro Press in the United States* (College Park, Md.: McGrath Publishing Co., 1968 reprint of 1922 ed.), 204.

Chapter One: The Birth of the Black Press

1. Lerone Bennett, Jr., *Pioneers in Protest* (Chicago: Johnson Publishing Co., 1968), 61.
2. Ibid.
3. Joel Williamson, *Origins of Segregation* (Boston: D.C. Heath and Company, 1968), 61–62.
4. I. Garland Penn, *The Afro-American Press and Its Editors* (New York: Arno Press and The New York Times Co., 1969 reprint of 1884 ed.), 18.
5. Bennett Jr., *Pioneers in Protest*, 61.
6. Ibid., 62.
7. William Loren Katz, *Eyewitness: The Negro in American History* (New York: Pitman Publishing Corporation, 1968), 171.
8. Wherton L. Dillon, *Slavery Attacked: Southern Slaves and Their Allies* (Baton Rouge: Louisiana University Press, 1990), 217.
9. Ibid., 220.

Chapter Two: The Struggle Against Slavery (1831–1841)

1. *Encyclopaedia Britannica*, 1969, "The Negro In American History, III: Slaves and Masters, 1567–1854," Mortimer J. Adler et al., eds, 270.
2. Ibid., 165.
3. Ibid., 251.
4. Penelope L. Bullock, *The Afro-American Periodical Press, 1838–1909* (Baton Rouge: Louisiana State University Press, 1981), 27.
5. Penn, *The Afro-American Press and Its Editors*, 60.
6. Bullock, *The Afro-American Press, 1838–1909*, 31.
7. Ibid., 27.
8. *Encyclopaedia Britannica*, "The Negro In American History, III: Slaves and Masters, 1567–1854," 219.
9. Ibid., 232.
10. Ibid., 206.
11. Ibid., 173.
12. Bullock, *The Afro-American Press, 1838–1909*, 31.
13. Ibid., 32.
14. Ibid.
15. Ibid.
16. Penn, *The Afro-American Press and Its Editors*, 32.
17. *Encyclopaedia Britannica*, "The Negro In American History, III: Slaves and Masters, 1567–1854," 206.
18. Ibid., 143.

Chapter Three: The Struggle Against Slavery (1842–1849)

1. Dillon, *Slavery Attacked: Southern Slaves and Their Allies, 1619–1865*, 208.
2. Ibid., 210.
3. Ibid., 214.
4. Ibid.
5. Penn, *The Afro-American Press and Its Editors*, 62.
6. Ibid., 63.
7. Carter R. Bryan, *Negro Journalism in America Before Emancipation* (Lexington, Ky.: The Association For Education in Journalism, University of Kentucky, Monograph #12, September 1969), 19.
8. Dillon, *Slavery Attacked: Southern Slaves and Their Allies, 1619–1865*, note, 219.

9. Samuel Eliot Morrison, *The Oxford History of the American People* (New York: Oxford University Press, 1965), 567.
10. Penn, *The Afro-American Press and Its Editors*, 64.
11. Dillon, *Slavery Attacked: Southern Slaves and Their Allies, 1619–1865*, 215.
12. Penn, *The Afro-American Press and Its Editors*, 65.
13. Morrison, *The Oxford History of the American People*, 568.
14. *Encyclopaedia Britannica*, "The Negro In American History, III: Slaves and Masters, 1567–1854," 103.

Chapter Four: Frederick Douglass and *The North Star*

1. Bryan, *Negro Journalism in America Before Emancipation*, 21.
2. Ibid.
3. Ibid.
4. Dillon, *Slavery Attacked: Southern Slaves and Their Allies, 1619–1865*, 229–230.
5. Ibid.
6. Katz, *Eyewitness: The Negro in American History*, 194.
7. Ibid., 189.
8. *Encyclopaedia Britannica*, "The Negro In American History, III: Slaves and Masters, 1567–1854," 66.
9. Katz, *Eyewitness: The Negro in American History*, 189.
10. Ibid.
11. *Encyclopaedia Britannica*, "The Negro in American History, III: Slaves and Masters, 1567–1854," 206.
12. Dillon, *Slavery Attacked: Southern Slaves and Their Allies, 1619–1865*, 216.
13. Lerone Bennett, Jr., *The Shaping of Black America*, (Chicago: Johnson Publishing Co., 1975), 131.

Chapter Five: Advocates and Abolitionists

1. Katz, *Eyewitness: The Negro In American History*, 191.
2. Dillon, *Slavery Attacked: Southern Slaves and Their Allies, 1619–1865*, 228.

3. Katz, *Eyewitness: The Negro In American History*, 199.
4. Ibid., 190.
5. Ibid., 187.
6. *Encyclopaedia Britannica*, "The Negro In American History, III: Slaves and Masters, 1567–1854," 54.
7. Katz, *Eyewitness: The Negro In American History*, 141.
8. *Encyclopaedia Britannica*, "The Negro In American History, III: Slaves and Masters, 1567–1854," III, 3.
9. Mary Frances Berry and John W. Blassingame, *Long Memory: The Black Experience in America*, (New York: Oxford, 1982), 399.
10. *Encyclopaedia Britannica*, "The Negro In American History, III: Slaves and Masters, 1567–1854," 7.
11. Katz, *Eyewitness: The Negro In American History*, 191.
12. Ibid.
13. Berry and Blassingame, *Long Memory: The Black Experience in America*, 143.
14. Katz, *Eyewitness: The Negro In American History*, 188.
15. Ibid.
16. *Encyclopaedia Britannica*, "The Negro In American History, II: A Taste of Freedom, 1854–1927," 425–426.
17. Dillon, *Slavery Attacked: Southern Slaves and Their Allies, 1619–1865*, 228.
18. Ibid., 229.
19. Harold Cruse, *The Crisis of the Negro Intellectual* (New York: William Morrow & Co., 1967), 5. However, George Shepperson, the source for Cruse's attribution of the phrase to Delany, is tentative: "For Delany, the only answer was 'Africa for the Africans.' With [Edward] Blyden, [Delany] appears to have been one of the first to have used this magnetic slogan." See George Shepperson, "Notes on Negro Influences on the Emergence of African Nationalism," *Journal of African History* 1 (1960) no. 2.
20. Dillon, *Slavery Attacked: Southern Slaves and Their Allies, 1619–1865*, 227.

Chapter Six: Civil War and Emancipation

1. Lerone Bennett, Jr., *The Shaping of Black America*, 173.
2. Ibid., 172.
3. Ibid.
4. Katz, *Eyewitness: The Negro In American History*, 207.
5. Dillon, *Slavery Attacked: Southern Slaves and Their Allies, 1619–1865*, 254.
6. Ibid., 255.
7. Ibid., 253.
8. Ibid., 257.
9. Ibid., 255.
10. Bullock, *The Afro-American Press, 1838–1909*, 55.
11. Carter R. Bryan, *Negro Journalism in America Before Emancipation*, 23.
12. Eric Foner, *Reconstruction: America's Unfinished Business, 1863–1877* (New York: Harper & Row, 1988), 63.
13. Ibid., 64.
14. Ibid.
15. Ibid., 36.
16. Ibid., 32.
17. Ibid., 31.
18. Ibid., 64.
19. Ibid., 65.
20. Penn, *The Afro-American Press and Its Editors*, 101.
21. Foner, *Reconstruction: America's Unfinished Business, 1863–1877*, 67.
22. Leslie H. Fishel, "The Negro in Northern Politics 1870–1900," in August Meier and Elliott Rudwick, eds., *The Making of Black America, Vol. 2* (New York: Atheneum, 1969), 57.

Chapter Seven: Reconstruction and the Black Press

1. John Hope Franklin, "History of Racial Segregation in the United States," Meier and Rudwick, eds. *The Making of Black America, Vol. 2*, 5.
2. Foner, *Reconstruction: America's Unfinished Business, 1863–1877*, 101–107 passim.
3. Herbert Shapiro, *White Violence and Black Re-*

sponse: From Reconstruction to Montgomery (Amherst: University of Massachusetts, 1988), 5.

4. Shapiro, *White Violence and Black Response: From Reconstruction to Montgomery*, 6.
5. Foner, *Reconstruction: America's Unfinished Business, 1863–1877*, 154.
6. Benjamin Quarles, *The Negro in the Making of America* (New York: Macmillan Publishing Co., 1987), 143.
7. George B. Tindall, "The Question of Race in The South Carolina Constitutional Convention of 1895," in August Meier and Elliott Rudwick, eds., *The Making of Black America, Vol. 2*, 51.
8. Ibid., Vernon L. Wharton, "The Race Issue in the Overthrow of Reconstruction of Mississippi," in August Meier and Elliott Rudwick, eds., *The Making of Black America, Vol. 2*, 375.
9. Ibid., 373.
10. Ibid., 374.
11. Ibid.
12. Ibid.
13. Bernard Mandel, "Samuel Gompers and the Negro Workers, 1886–1914," 75.

Chapter Eight: The Crusader—T. Thomas Fortune

1. Perry J. Ashley, ed., *Dictionary of Literary Biography*, Vol. 43, American Newspaper Journalism, 1690–1872. Detroit, Mich.: Gale Research Co., 1985.
2. Ibid.
3. Ibid.
4. Ibid.
5. Ibid.
6. Ibid.
7. Ibid.
8. John Hope Franklin, *From Slavery to Freedom: A History of Negro Americans*, 3rd edition (New York: Random House), 214–241.
9. John Hope Franklin, "History of Racial Segregation in the United States," Meier and Rudwick, eds. *The Making of Black America, Vol. 2*, 8.

10. Shapiro, *White Violence and Black Response: From Reconstruction to Montgomery*, 36.
11. Ashley, ed., *Dictionary of Literary Biography, Vol. 43, American Newspaper Journalism, 1690–1872.*
12. Roland E. Wolseley, *The Black Press, U.S.A.* (Ames, Iowa: University of Iowa Press, 1971), 48.
13. George M. Frederickson, *The Black Image in the White Mind* (New York: Harper & Row, 1971), 276.
14. Ashley, ed., *Dictionary of Literary Biography, Vol. 43, American Newspaper Journalism, 1690–1872.*

Chapter Nine: Giant of Advocacy Journalism—Ida B. Wells

1. Alfreda M. Duster, ed., *Crusade For Justice: The Autobiography of Ida B. Wells* (Chicago: University of Chicago Press), 1970.
2. Ibid.
3. Ibid.
4. Ibid.
5. *Encyclopaedia Britannica*, "The Negro In American History, III: Slaves and Masters, 1567–1854," 173.

Chapter Ten: Radicals and Nationalists

1. Howard N. Rabinowitz, *Race Relations in the Urban South, 1865–1890* (New York: Oxford University Press), 234–235.
2. Ibid.
3. Ibid.
4. Stephen R. Fox, *The Guardian of Boston: William Monroe Trotter* (New York: Atheneum, 1970), 20.
5. Ibid., 216.
6. Frederickson, *The Black Image in the White Mind*, 280.
7. Ibid., 281.
8. Fox, *The Guardian of Boston: William Monroe Trotter*, 190.
9. Rabinowitz, *Race Relations in the Urban South, 1865–1890*, 236.
10. Ibid., 237.
11. Ibid.

12. Francis L. Broderick, *W. E. B. DuBois: Negro Leader in a Time of Crisis* (Stanford, Calif.: Stanford University Press, 1959) 1–5; cf. Lerone Bennett, Jr. *Pioneers in Protest* (Baltimore, Md.: Penguin Books, 1969), 244.
13. Bennett, Jr., *Pioneers in Protest*, 238.
14. Howard Zinn, *The Twentieth Century: A People's History* (New York: Harper & Row, 1984).
15. Fox, *The Guardian of Boston: William Monroe Trotter*; W. E. B. Du Bois, "The African Roots of War," *The Atlantic*, May 1915.
16. Fox, *The Guardian of Boston: William Monroe Trotter*.

Chapter Eleven: The *Chicago Daily Defender* and the *Pittsburgh Courier*

1. Zinn, *The Twentieth Century: A People's History*.
2. Roi Ottley, *The Lonely Warrior: The Life and Times of Robert S. Abbott* (Chicago: Henry Regnery Co., 1955).
3. Ibid.
4. Ibid.
5. Ibid.
6. Ibid.
7. Ibid.
8. Ibid.
9. Ibid.
10. Metz Lochard, "Robert S. Abbott: Race Leader," *Phylon*, 8, 2 (1946), 124.
11. Andrew Buni, *Robert L. Vann of the Pittsburgh Courier* (Pittsburgh: University of Pittsburgh Press, 1974).

Chapter Twelve: After World War I: Marcus Garvey

1. David E. Cronon, *Black Moses: The Story of Marcus Garvey and The Universal Negro Improvement Association* (Lansing: University of Wisconsin Press, 1970).
2. Ibid.
3. Ibid.
4. Ibid.
5. Shapiro, *White Violence and Black Response: From Reconstruction to Montgomery*, 170.

Chapter Thirteen: World War II

1. Shapiro, *White Violence and Black Response: From Reconstruction to Montgomery*, 150.
2. Ibid., 188.
3. John D. Stevens, *From the Back of The Foxhole: Black Correspondents in World War II* (Lexington, Ky.: Department of Journalism, University of Kentucky, Association for Education in Journalism, 1973).
4. Ernest E. Jones, "The Washington News Beat," *Phylon*, 1946, 2nd Quarter, V II, N. 2, pp 127–128.
5. J. Kirk Sale, "The Amsterdam News: Black Is . . ." *The New York Times Sunday Magazine*, Feb. 9, 1969: 30.
6. Roland E. Wolseley, *The Black Press, U.S.A.* (Ames, Iowa: University of Iowa Press, 1971), 1st edition; cf. p. 272 of Wolseley's 1990 2nd edition, condensing the seven reasons into three broad statements.

Chapter Fourteen: A Black Journalism Empire

1. Roland E. Wolseley, *The Black Press, U.S.A.* (Ames, Iowa: University of Iowa Press, 1990), 86.
2. Ibid.
3. Seth Mydans, "Black Journalists Look to Last Ceiling," *The New York Times*, August 3, 1990: A16.

Chapter Fifteen: Black Liberation

1. Jannette L. Dates, "Print News," in *Split Image: African Americans in the Mass Media*, eds., Jannette L. Dates and William Barlow (Washington, D.C.: Howard University Press, 1992), 364.
2. Ibid.

Chapter Sixteen: Toward the Twenty-First Century

1. Jonathan P. Hicks, "More New Magazines and These Beckon To Black Readers," *The New York Times*, August 5, 1990: E20.
2. Ibid.
3. Roland E. Wolseley, *The Black Press, U.S.A.* (Ames, Iowa: University of Iowa Press, 1990), 212.

FOR FURTHER READING

Bennett, Lerone, Jr. *Pioneers in Protest*. Chicago: Johnson Publishing, 1968.

Bogle, Donald. *Toms, Coons, Mulattoes, Mammies and Bucks: An Interpretive History of Blacks in American Films*. New York: Viking Press, 1973.

Buni, Andrew. *Robert L. Vann of* The Pittsburgh Courier. Pittsburgh: University of Pittsburgh Press, 1974.

Cruse, Harold. *The Crisis of the Negro Intellectual*. New York: William Morrow, 1967.

Foner, Eric. *Reconstruction: America's Unfinished Revolution, 1863–1877*. New York: Harper & Row, 1988.

Franklin, John Hope. *From Slavery to Freedom: A History of Negro Americans*. 5th ed. New York: Alfred A. Knopf, 1980.

Horne, Gerald. *Black and Red: W. E. B. DuBois and the Afro-American Response to the Cold War, 1944–1963*. Albany: State University of New York Press, 1986.

Johnson, John H., and Lerone Bennett, Jr. *Succeeding Against the Odds*. New York: Warner Books, 1989.

Lerner, Gerda. *Black Women in White America: A Documentary History*. New York: Random House, 1972.

Lincoln, C. Eric. *The Black Muslims in America*. Boston: Beacon Press, 1973.

Meier, August, and Elliott Rudwick, eds. *The Making of Black America.* 2 vols. New York: Atheneum, 1969.

Shapiro, Herbert. *White Violence and Black Response: From Reconstruction to Montgomery.* Amherst: University of Massachusetts Press, 1988.

Williams, Juan. *Eyes on the Prize: America's Civil Rights Years, 1954–1965.* New York: Viking Penguin, 1987.

Zinn, Howard. *A People's History of the United States.* New York: Harper & Row, 1981.

————. *The Twentieth Century: A People's History.* New York: Harper & Row, 1984.

A comprehensive list of contemporary black journalists and publishers, and the roles of blacks in film, book publishing, drama, the recording industry, advertising, television, and radio, are subjects well beyond the scope of this brief history.

Yet the story of blacks in other media is as compelling a story of human endeavor as any described here. A number of excellent studies have been published on black cultural developments in the press related media. Among the best are Thomas Cripps's *Slow Fade to Black: The Negro in American Film, 1900–1942* (1976) and *Black Film as Genre* (1978); Donald Bogle's *Toms, Coons, Mulattoes, Mammies and Bucks* (1973); Daniel Leab's *From Sambo to Superspade: The Black Experience in Motion Pictures* (1975); Gary Null's *Black Hollywood: The Black Performer in Motion Pictures* (1975); and James R. Nesteby's *Black Images in American Films 1896–1954: The Interplay Between Civil Rights and Film Culture* (1978). For a comprehensive and highly readable account of the growth of black radio stations, the Black networks, and the growth of the black commercial recording industry, readers ought to consult *Split Image: African Americans in the Mass Media*, edited by Jannette L. Dates and William Barlow (1990).

INDEX